GRAPHIC LIBRARY

GREAT ESCAPES OF WORLD WAR II

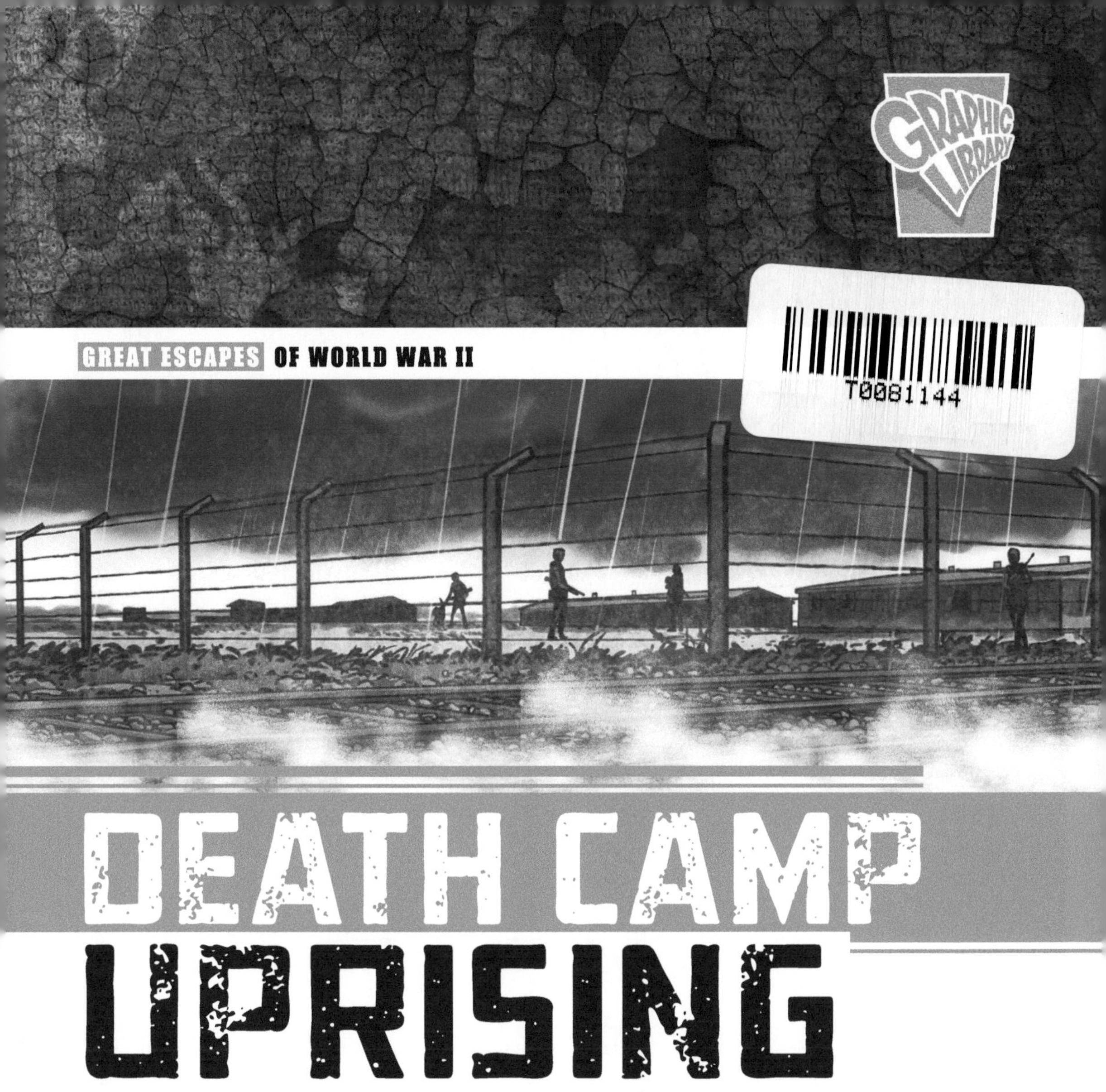

DEATH CAMP UPRISING

THE ESCAPE FROM SOBIBOR CONCENTRATION CAMP

by Nel Yomtov

CAPSTONE PRESS
a capstone imprint

Graphic Library is published by Capstone Press,
1710 Roe Crest Drive, North Mankato, Minnesota 56003
www.mycapstone.com

Library of Congress Cataloging-in-Publication data is available on the Library of Congress website.
ISBN 978-1-5157-3532-8 (library binding)
ISBN 978-1-5157-3537-3 (paperback)
ISBN 978-1-5157-3549-6 (eBook PDF)

Editor
Anna Butzer

Art Director
Nathan Gassman

Designer
Ted Williams

Media Researcher
Wanda Winch

Production Specialist
Gene Bentdahl

Illustrator
Wilson Tortosa

Colorist
Michael Bartolo

Design Element: Shutterstock: aodaodaodaod, paper texture, esfera,
map design, Natalya Kalyatina, barbed wire design

Printed in the United States   5335

TABLE OF CONTENTS

CONDEMNED TO DIE

The Sobibor death camp, or concentration camp, was located in the village of Sobibor, near the eastern border of Poland. During World War II (1939–1945), Poland was occupied by Nazi Germany. The camp was built to imprison and then execute Jews from Europe, including Poland, the Netherlands, and the Soviet Union.

Sobibor was one of three similar death camps in Poland. The three killing centers were part of a Nazi scheme called Operation Reinhard. The goal of this operation was to murder every Jew in Nazi-occupied Poland. The killings at Sobibor began in May 1942. In all, about 1.7 million Jewish people were murdered during Operation Reinhard.

Entire villages of Jews were rounded up and transported by railway to Sobibor. When they arrived, the people were stripped of all their belongings, including their clothing and jewelry. Men and women were separated. Most of the new arrivals were immediately sent to gas chambers. There they were murdered using carbon monoxide gas — the same poisonous gas that comes from a car exhaust. Hundreds of others were shot or beaten to death.

Some captives were put to work by the Nazis as tailors, goldsmiths, shoemakers, and other tasks. Many were required to remove the dead bodies of their fellow Jews from the gas chambers and then burn them.

The Nazis kept their death camps very secretive. New arrivals had no knowledge of the terrible fate that awaited them. In addition, the outside world knew little about the organized mass murder of Jews.

Condemned to certain death, however, the Jewish prisoners at Sobibor secretly planned a mass escape. But how would they do this? The German guards at the camp were heavily armed with rifles and machine guns. Capture meant immediate execution. Any plan had little chance of success.

But even the risk of death was better than such a horrible existence.

RUSH TO FREEDOM

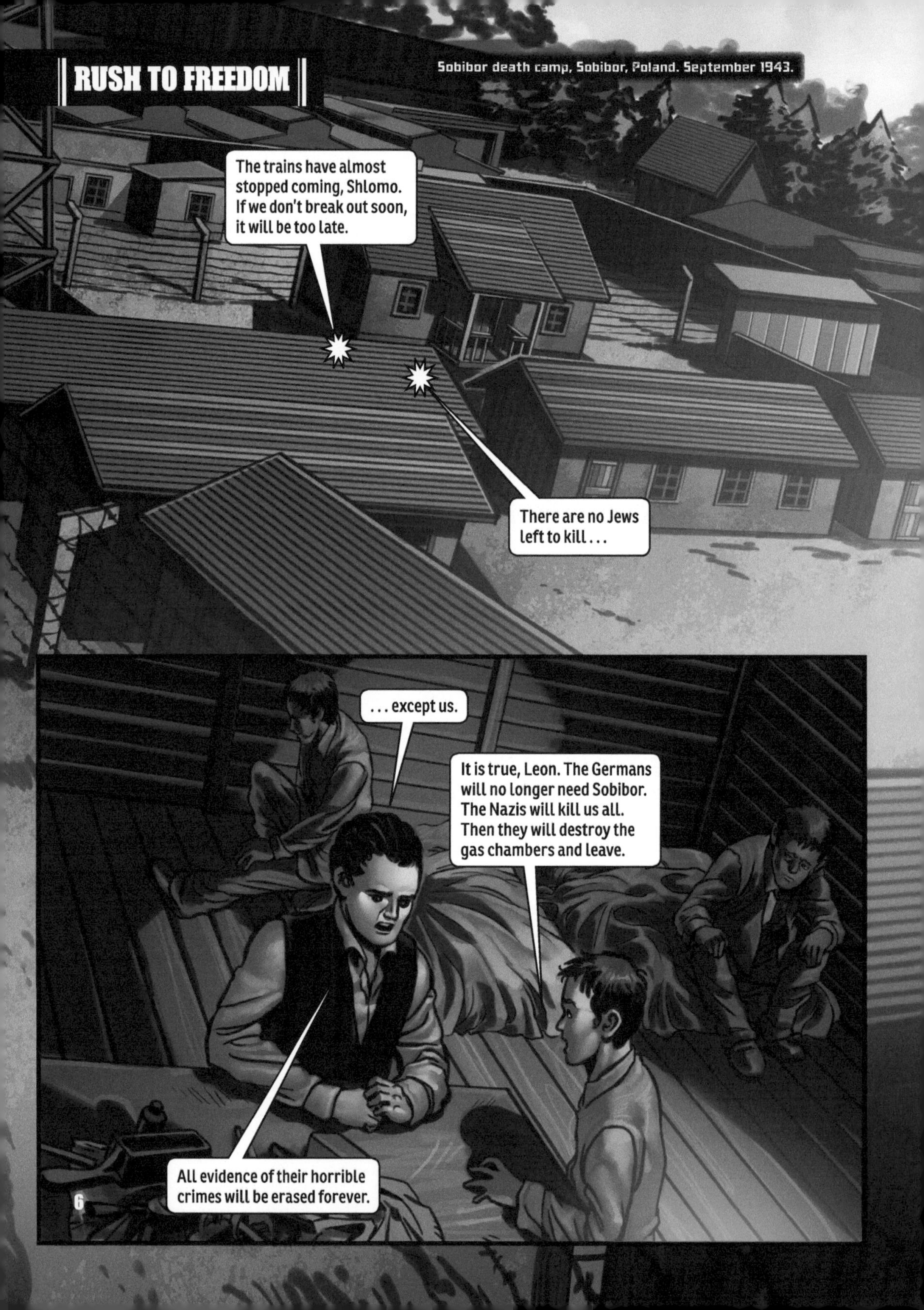
Sobibor death camp, Sobibor, Poland. September 1943.
The trains have almost stopped coming, Shlomo. If we don't break out soon, it will be too late.
There are no Jews left to kill . . .
. . . except us.
It is true, Leon. The Germans will no longer need Sobibor. The Nazis will kill us all. Then they will destroy the gas chambers and leave.
All evidence of their horrible crimes will be erased forever.

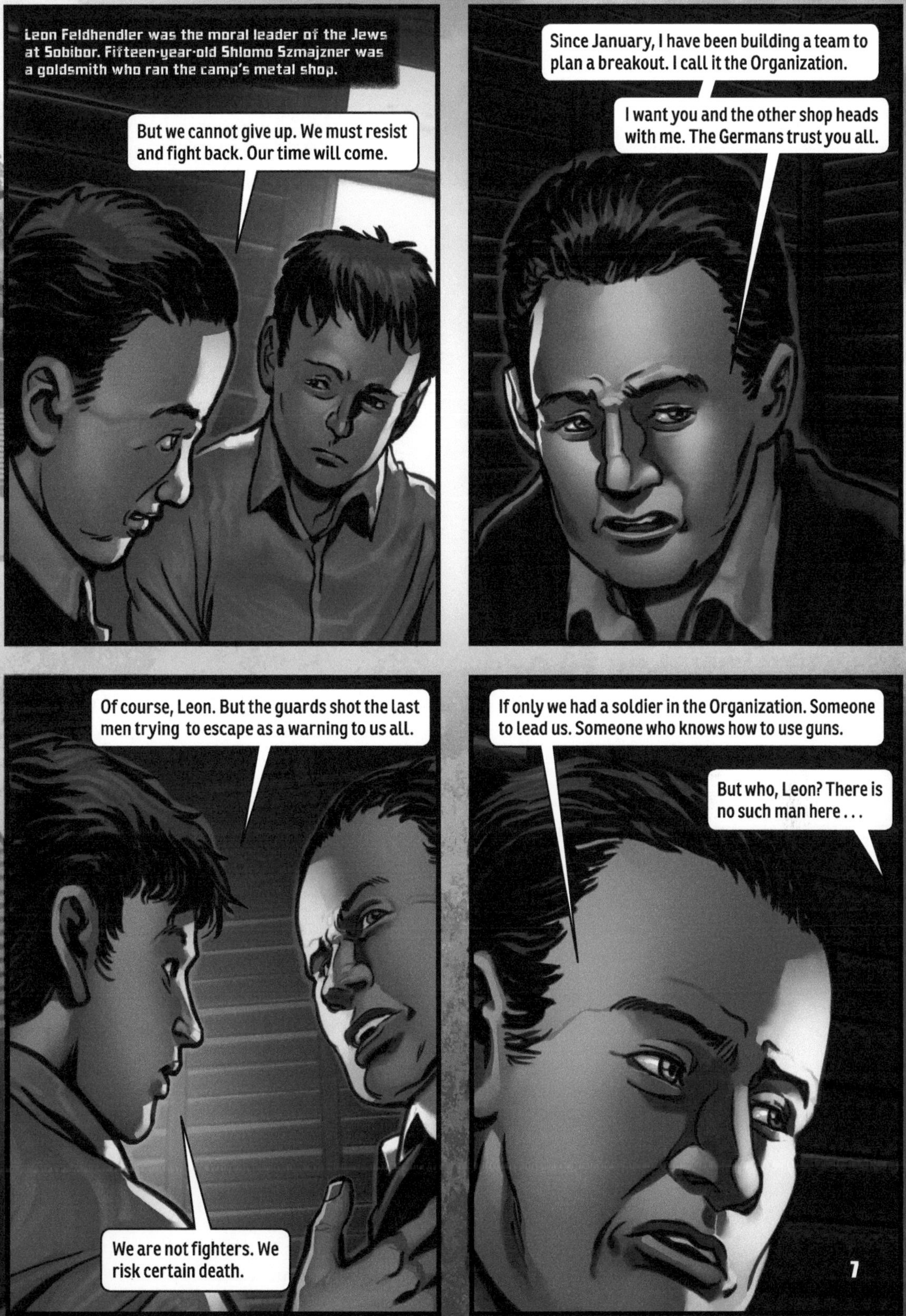
Leon Feldhendler was the moral leader of the Jews at Sobibor. Fifteen-year-old Shlomo Szmajzner was a goldsmith who ran the camp's metal shop.
But we cannot give up. We must resist and fight back. Our time will come.
Since January, I have been building a team to plan a breakout. I call it the Organization.
I want you and the other shop heads with me. The Germans trust you all.
Of course, Leon. But the guards shot the last men trying to escape as a warning to us all.
We are not fighters. We risk certain death.
If only we had a soldier in the Organization. Someone to lead us. Someone who knows how to use guns.
But who, Leon? There is no such man here . . .

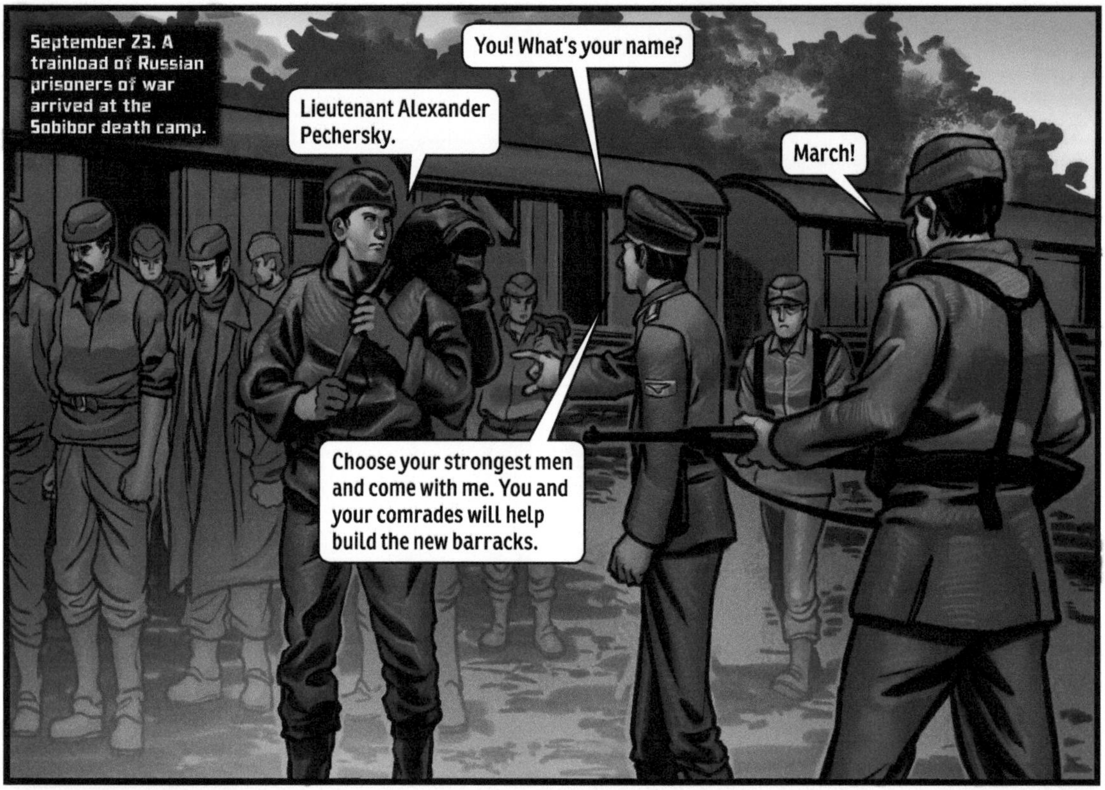
September 23. A trainload of Russian prisoners of war arrived at the Sobibor death camp.
You! What's your name?
Lieutenant Alexander Pechersky.
Choose your strongest men and come with me. You and your comrades will help build the new barracks.
March!

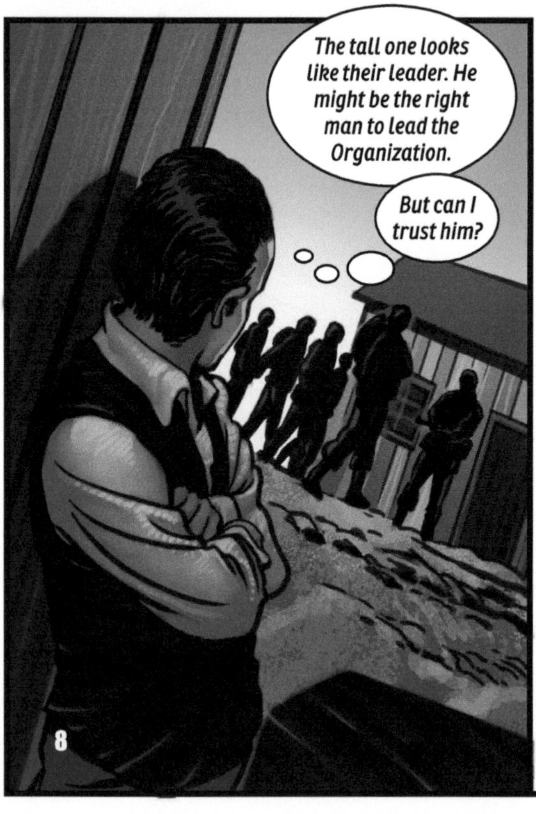
The tall one looks like their leader. He might be the right man to lead the Organization.
But can I trust him?

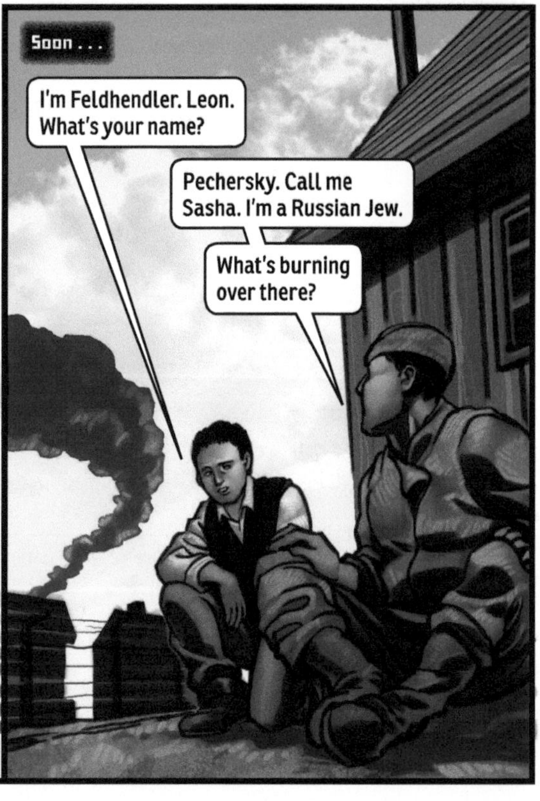
Soon . . .
I'm Feldhendler. Leon. What's your name?
Pechersky. Call me Sasha. I'm a Russian Jew.
What's burning over there?

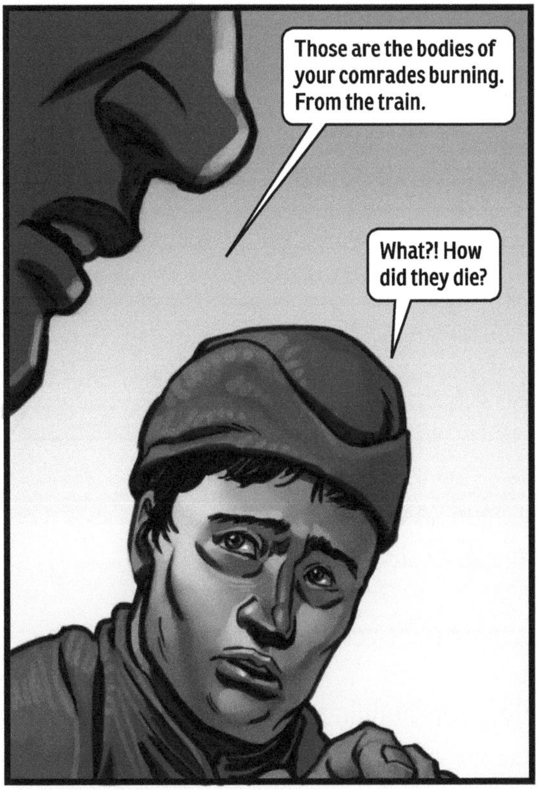
Those are the bodies of your comrades burning. From the train.
What?! How did they die?

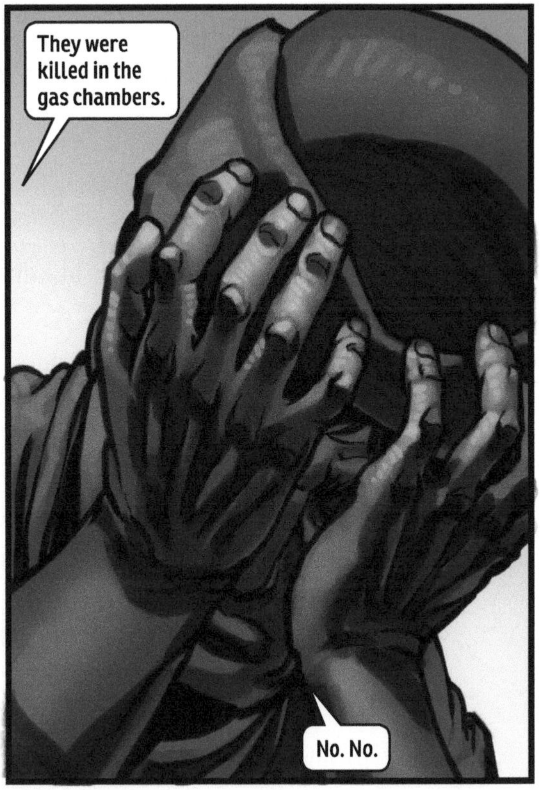
They were killed in the gas chambers.
No. No.

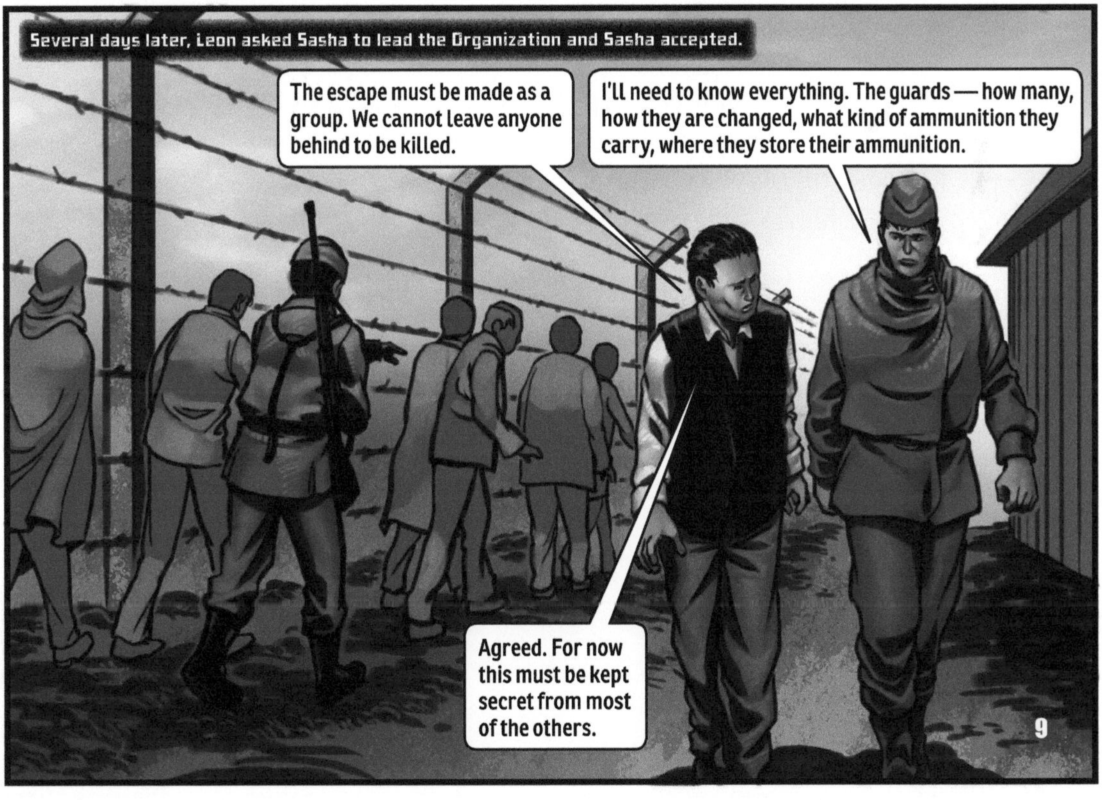
Several days later, Leon asked Sasha to lead the Organization and Sasha accepted.
The escape must be made as a group. We cannot leave anyone behind to be killed.
I'll need to know everything. The guards — how many, how they are changed, what kind of ammunition they carry, where they store their ammunition.
Agreed. For now this must be kept secret from most of the others.

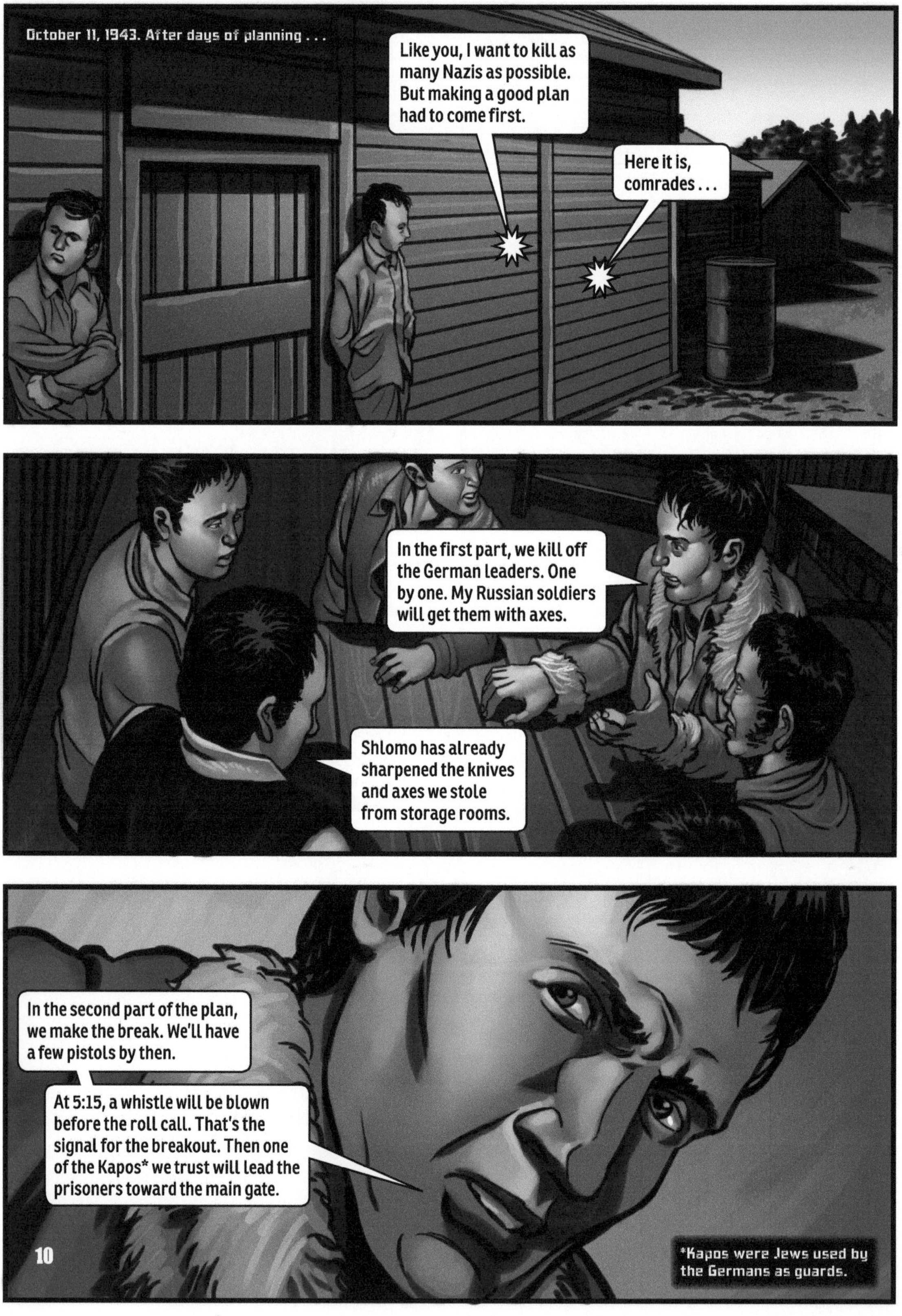
October 11, 1943. After days of planning . . .
Like you, I want to kill as many Nazis as possible. But making a good plan had to come first.
Here it is, comrades . . .
In the first part, we kill off the German leaders. One by one. My Russian soldiers will get them with axes.
Shlomo has already sharpened the knives and axes we stole from storage rooms.
In the second part of the plan, we make the break. We'll have a few pistols by then.
At 5:15, a whistle will be blown before the roll call. That's the signal for the breakout. Then one of the Kapos* we trust will lead the prisoners toward the main gate.
*Kapos were Jews used by the Germans as guards.

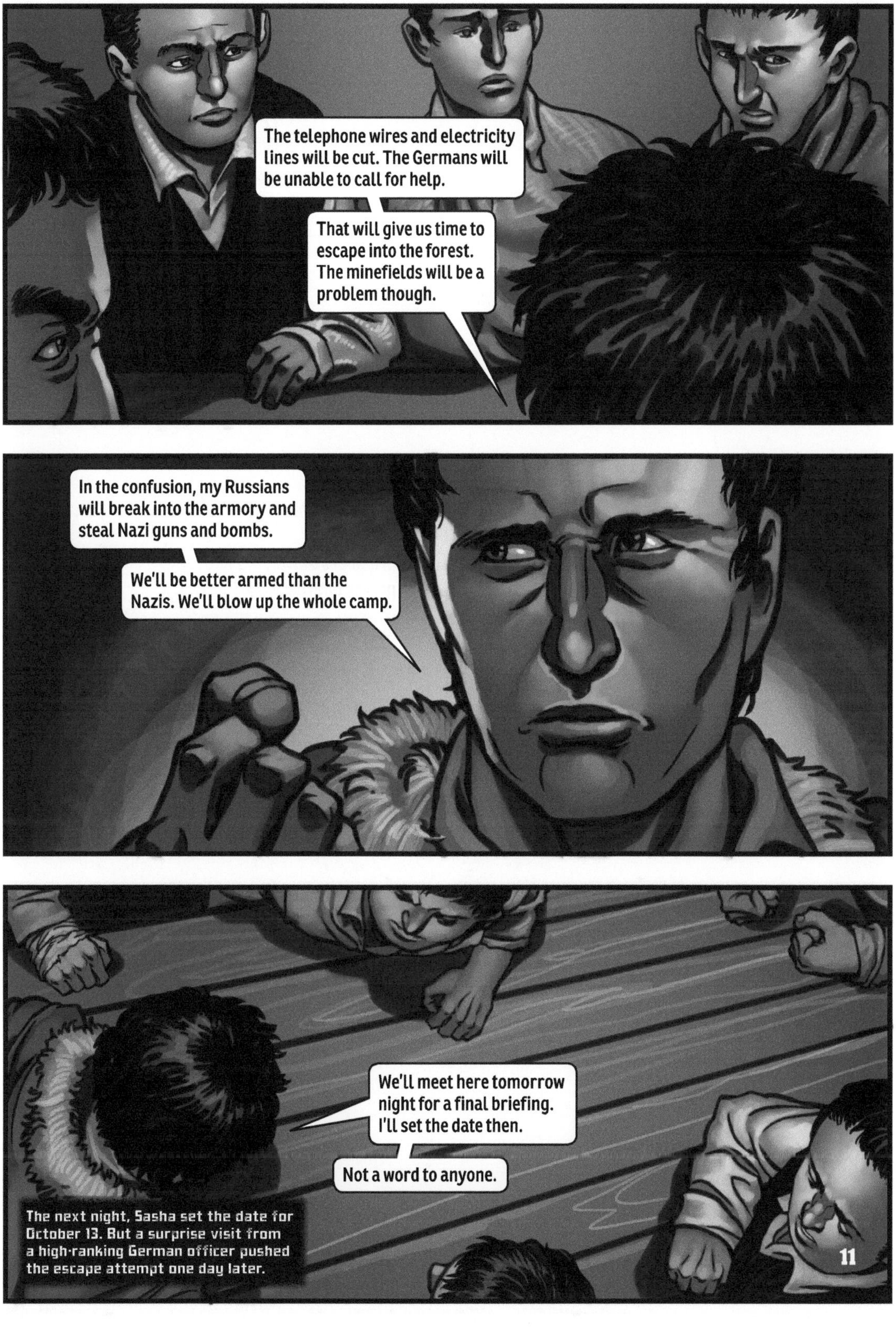
The telephone wires and electricity lines will be cut. The Germans will be unable to call for help.
That will give us time to escape into the forest. The minefields will be a problem though.
In the confusion, my Russians will break into the armory and steal Nazi guns and bombs.
We'll be better armed than the Nazis. We'll blow up the whole camp.
We'll meet here tomorrow night for a final briefing. I'll set the date then.
Not a word to anyone.
The next night, Sasha set the date for October 13. But a surprise visit from a high-ranking German officer pushed the escape attempt one day later.

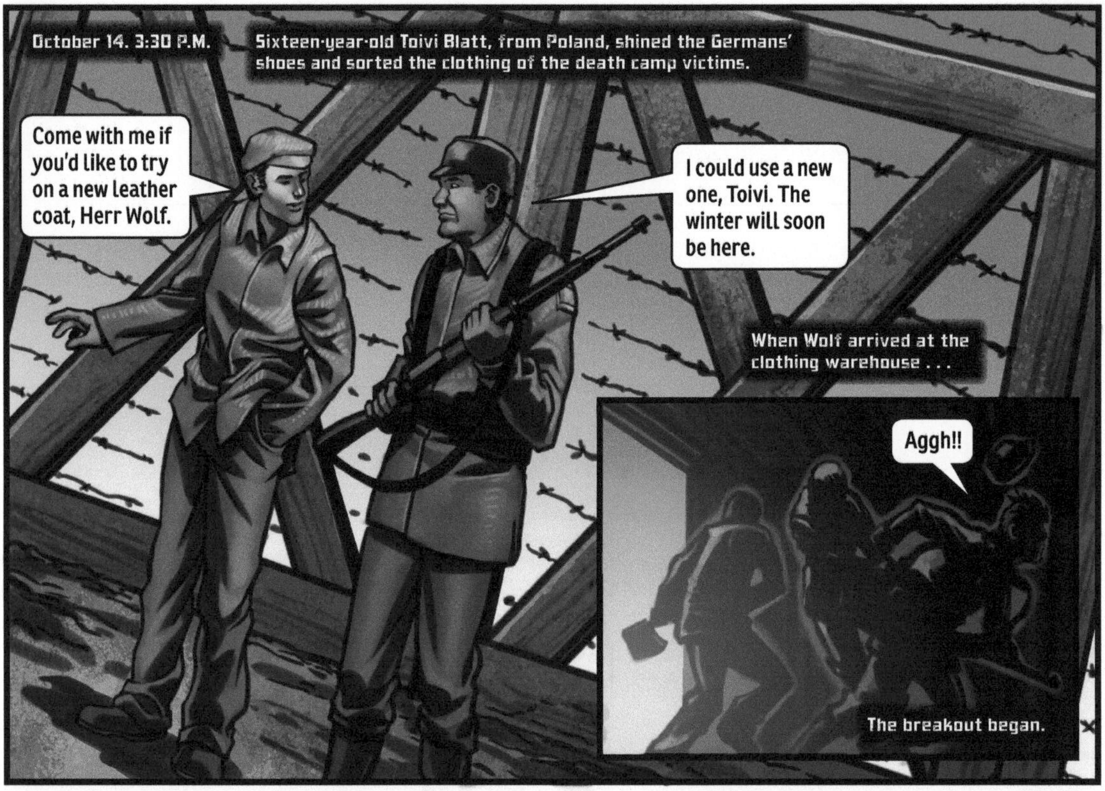
October 14. 3:30 P.M.
Sixteen-year-old Toivi Blatt, from Poland, shined the Germans' shoes and sorted the clothing of the death camp victims.
Come with me if you'd like to try on a new leather coat, Herr Wolf.
I could use a new one, Toivi. The winter will soon be here.
When Wolf arrived at the clothing warehouse . . .
Aggh!!
The breakout began.

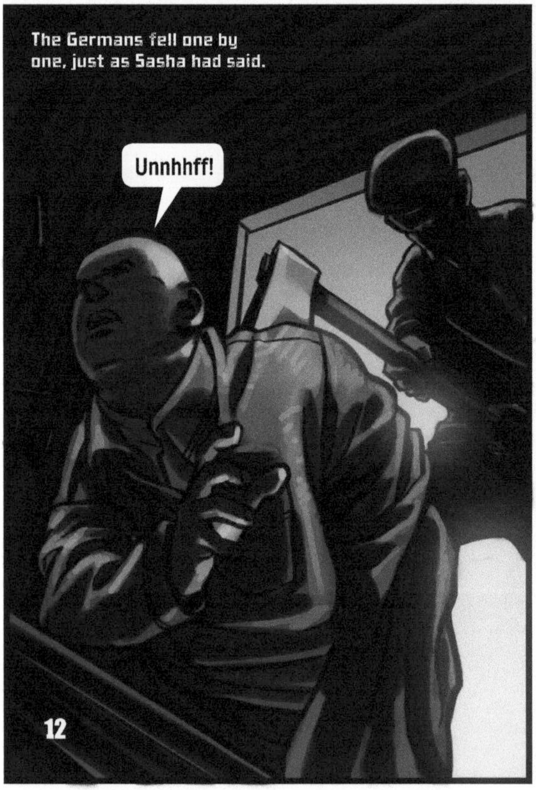
The Germans fell one by one, just as Sasha had said.
Unnhhff!

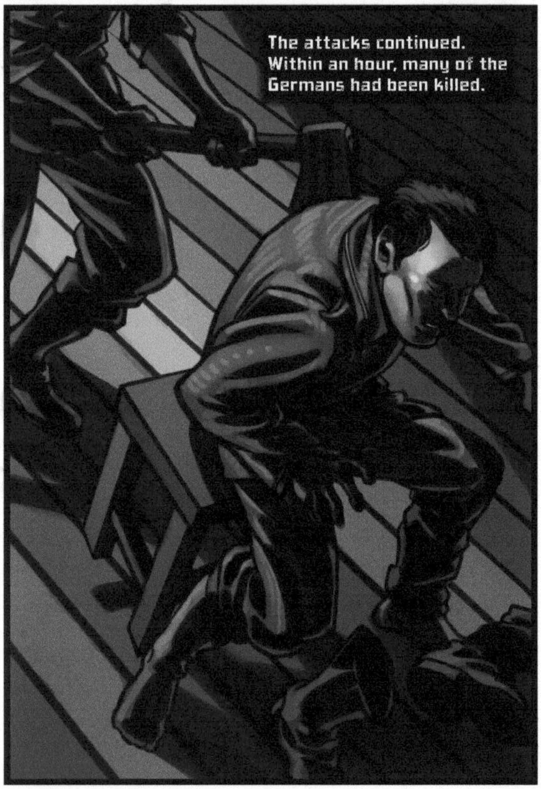
The attacks continued. Within an hour, many of the Germans had been killed.

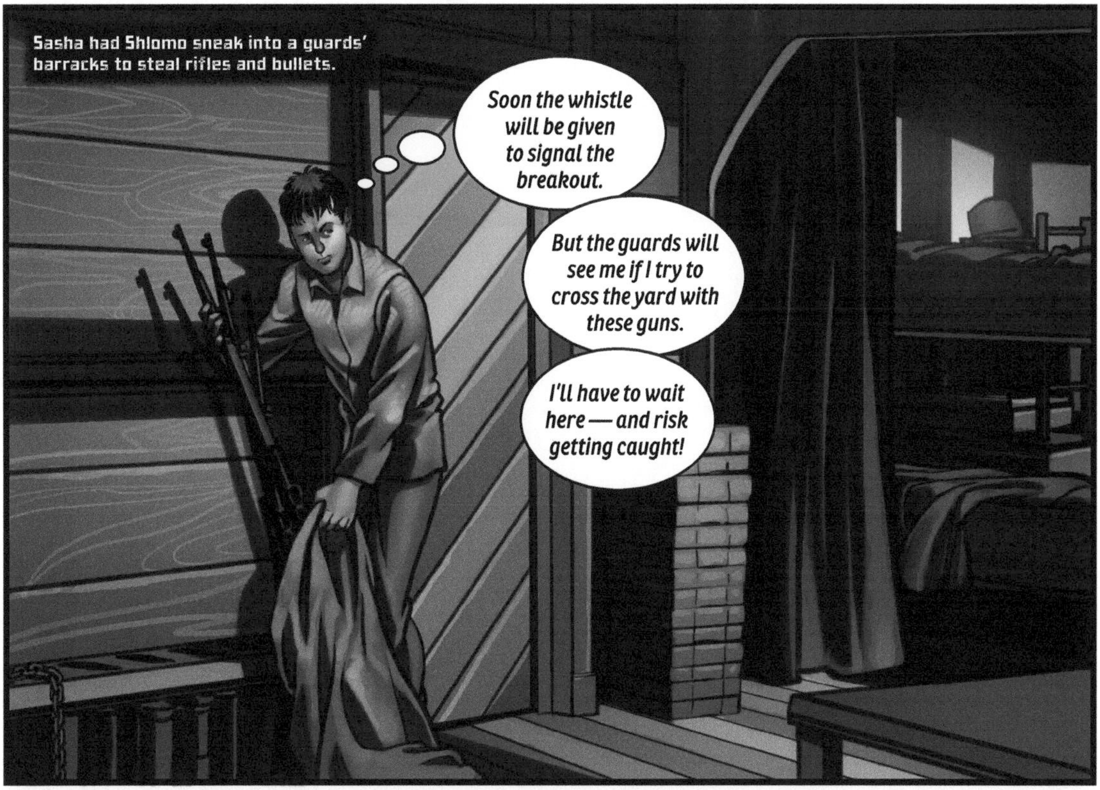
Sasha had Shlomo sneak into a guards' barracks to steal rifles and bullets.
Soon the whistle will be given to signal the breakout.
But the guards will see me if I try to cross the yard with these guns.
I'll have to wait here — and risk getting caught!

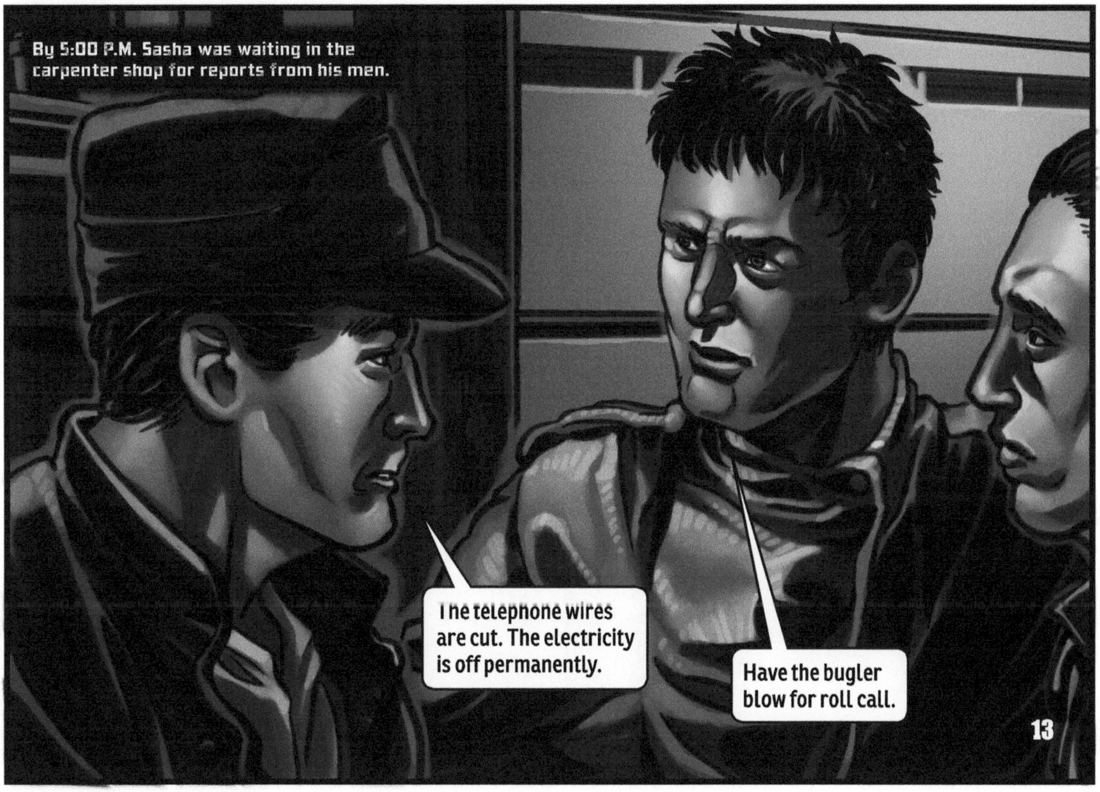
By 5:00 P.M. Sasha was waiting in the carpenter shop for reports from his men.
The telephone wires are cut. The electricity is off permanently.
Have the bugler blow for roll call.

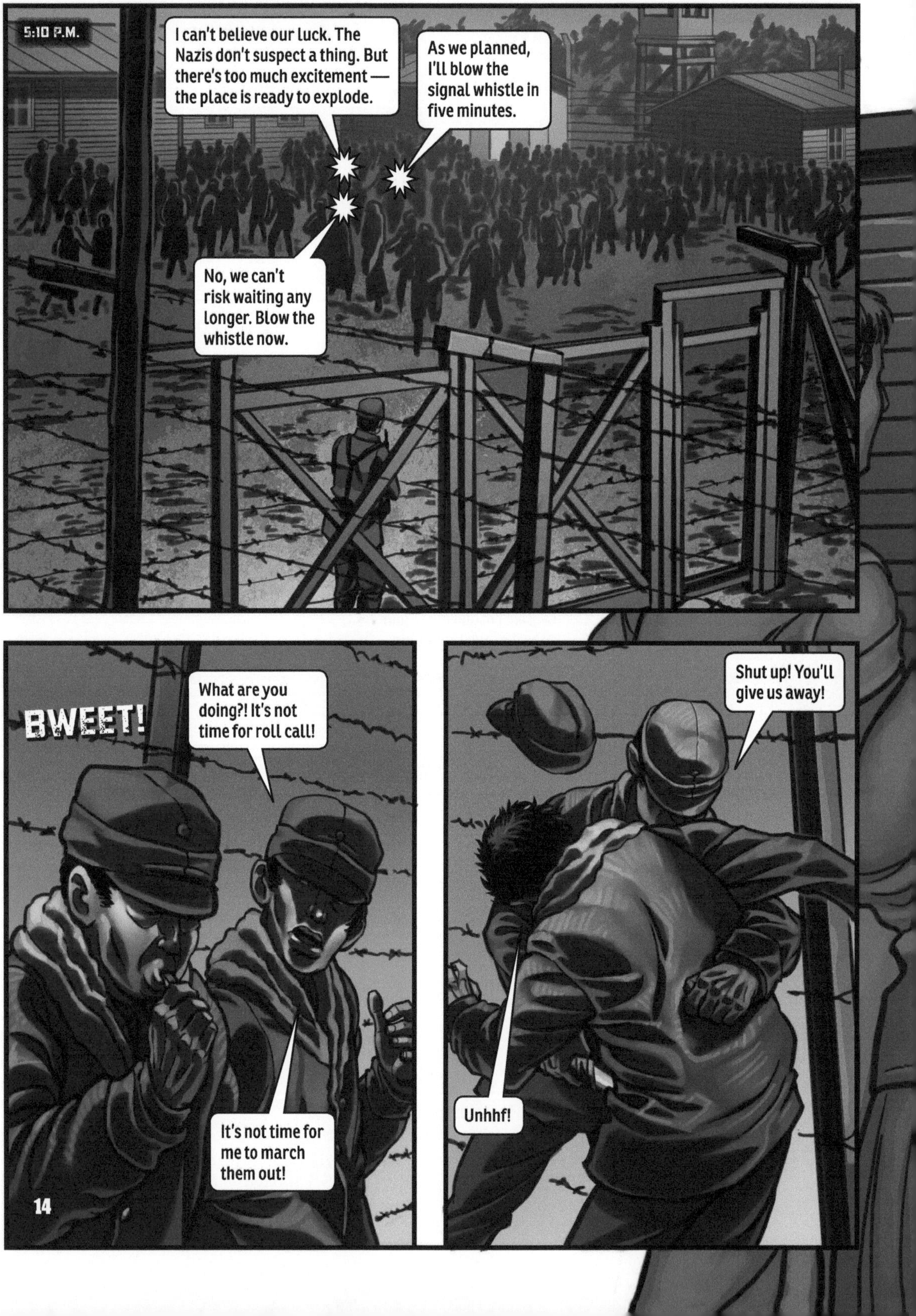
5:10 P.M.
I can't believe our luck. The Nazis don't suspect a thing. But there's too much excitement — the place is ready to explode.
As we planned, I'll blow the signal whistle in five minutes.
No, we can't risk waiting any longer. Blow the whistle now.
BWEET!
What are you doing?! It's not time for roll call!
It's not time for me to march them out!
Shut up! You'll give us away!
Unhhf!

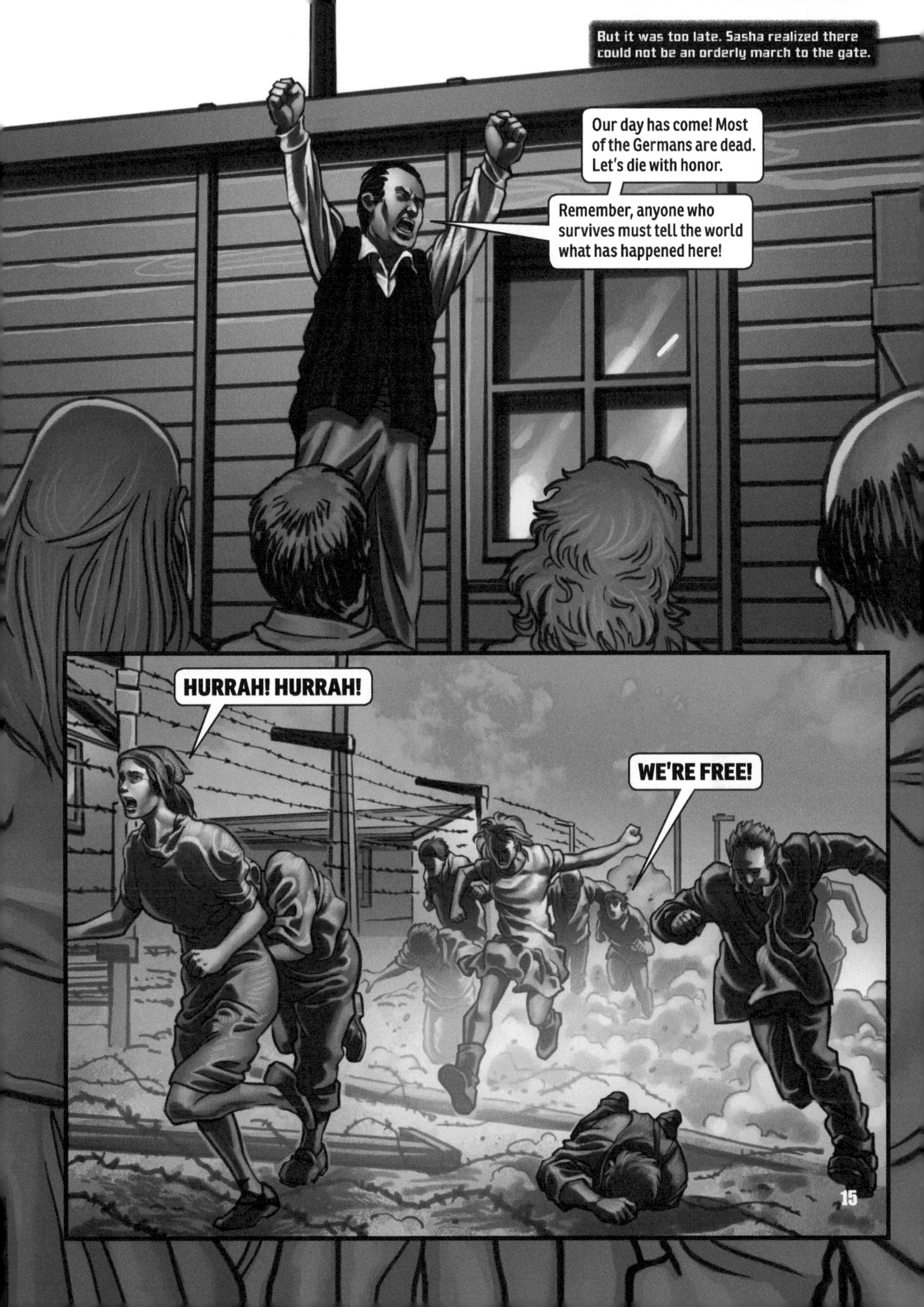
But it was too late. Sasha realized there could not be an orderly march to the gate.
Our day has come! Most of the Germans are dead. Let's die with honor.
Remember, anyone who survives must tell the world what has happened here!
HURRAH! HURRAH!
WE'RE FREE!

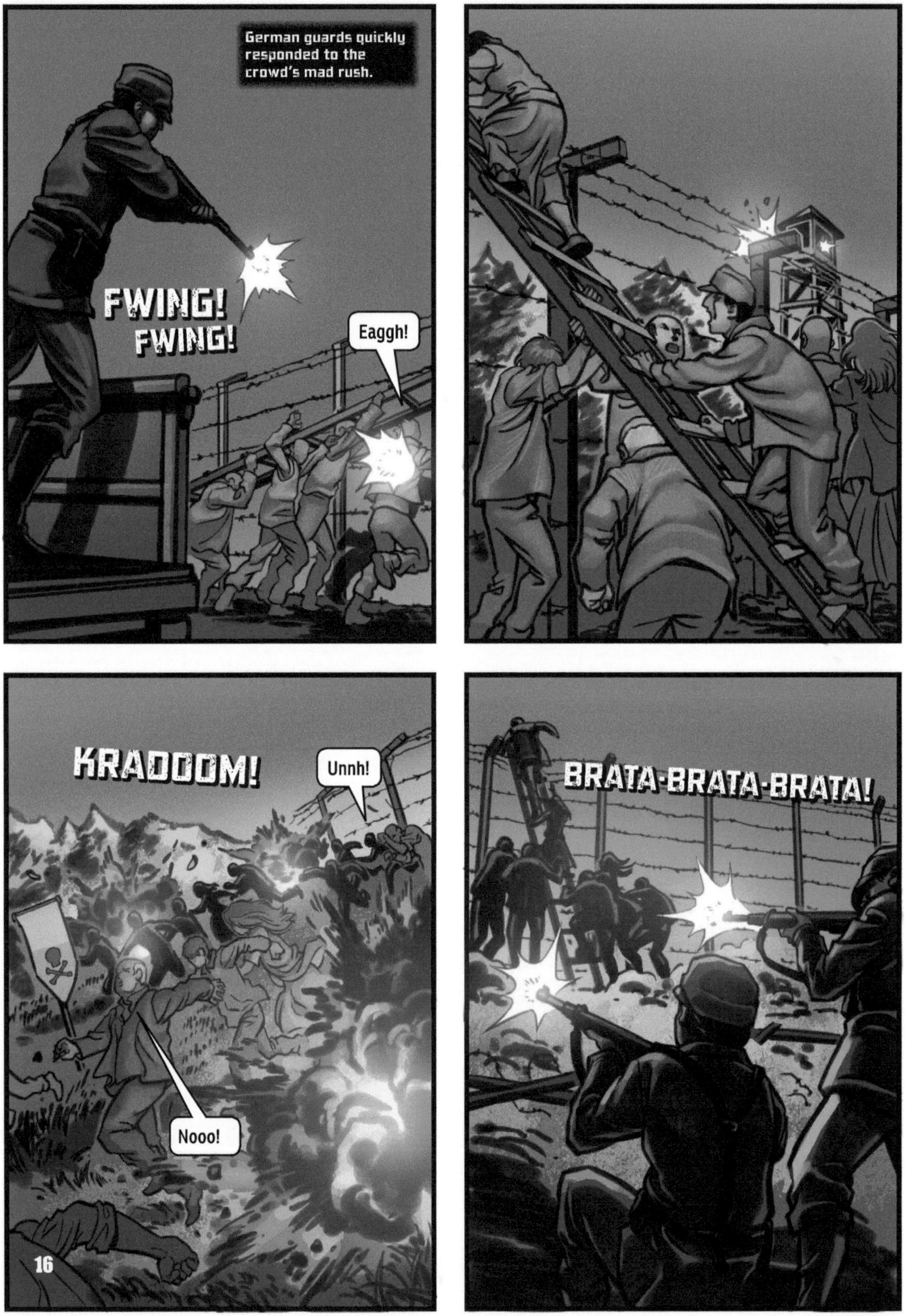
German guards quickly responded to the crowd's mad rush.
FWING! FWING!
Eaggh!
KRADOOM!
Unnh!
Nooo!
BRATA-BRATA-BRATA!

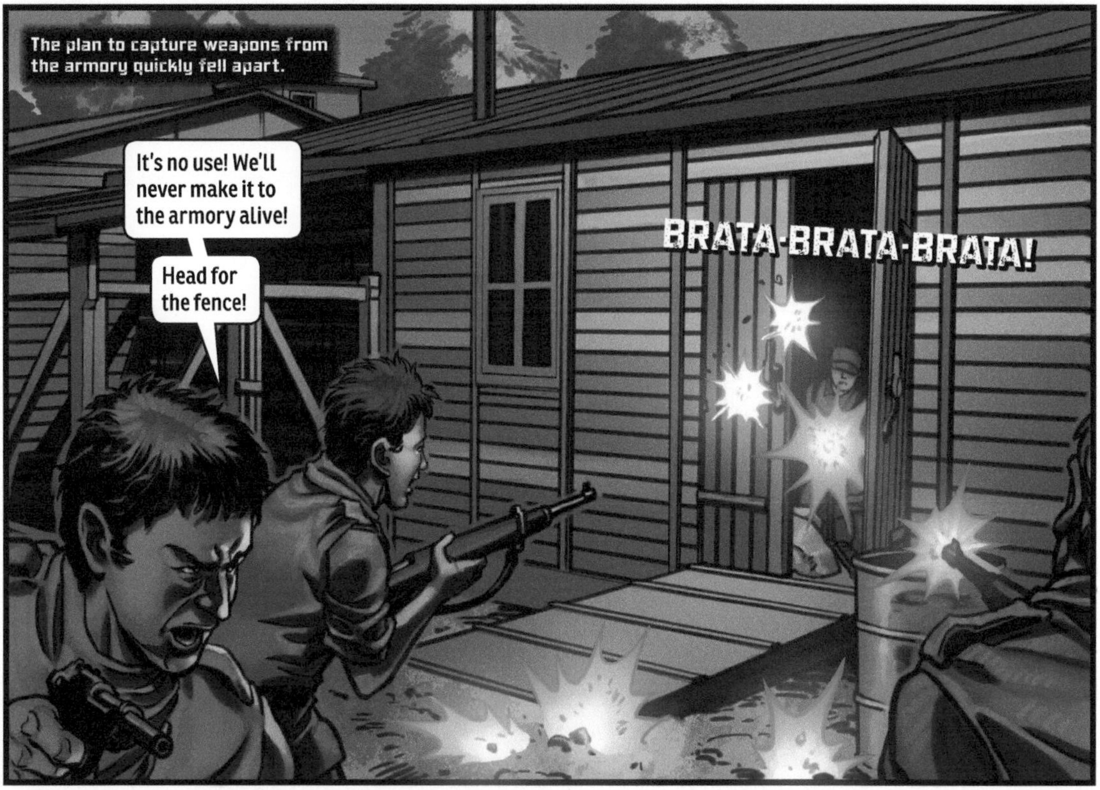
The plan to capture weapons from the armory quickly fell apart.
It's no use! We'll never make it to the armory alive!
Head for the fence!
BRATA-BRATA-BRATA!

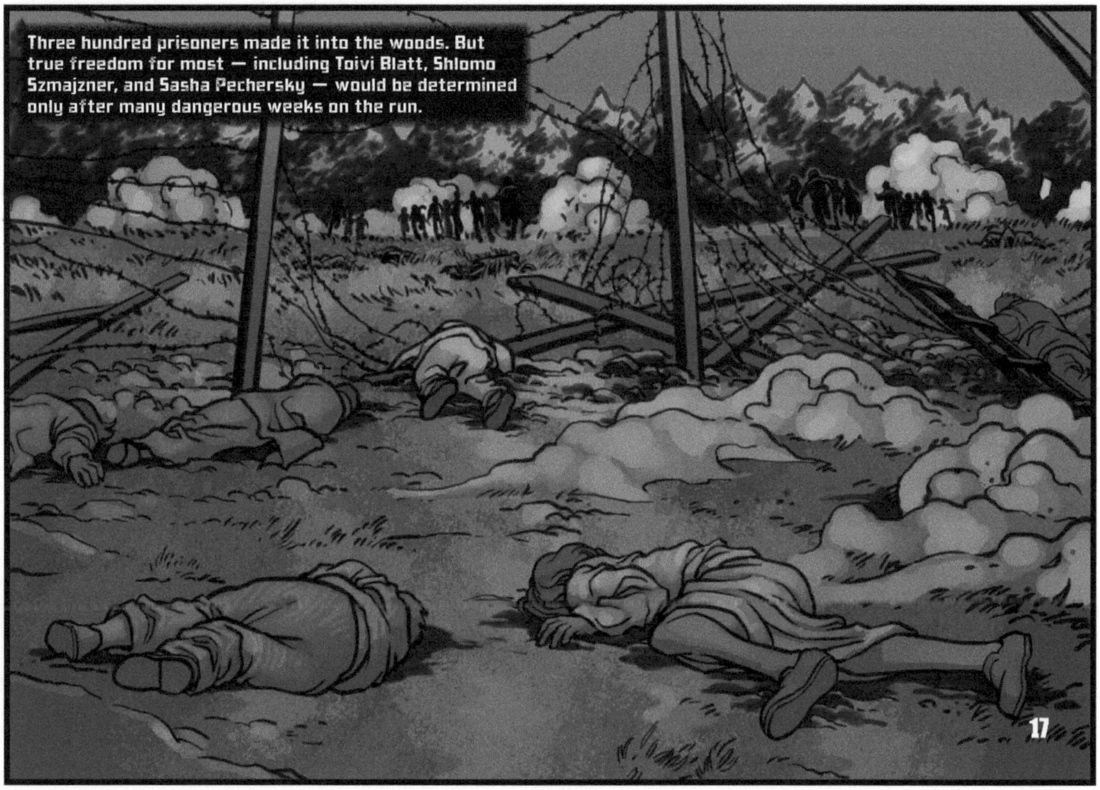
Three hundred prisoners made it into the woods. But true freedom for most — including Toivi Blatt, Shlomo Szmajzner, and Sasha Pechersky — would be determined only after many dangerous weeks on the run.

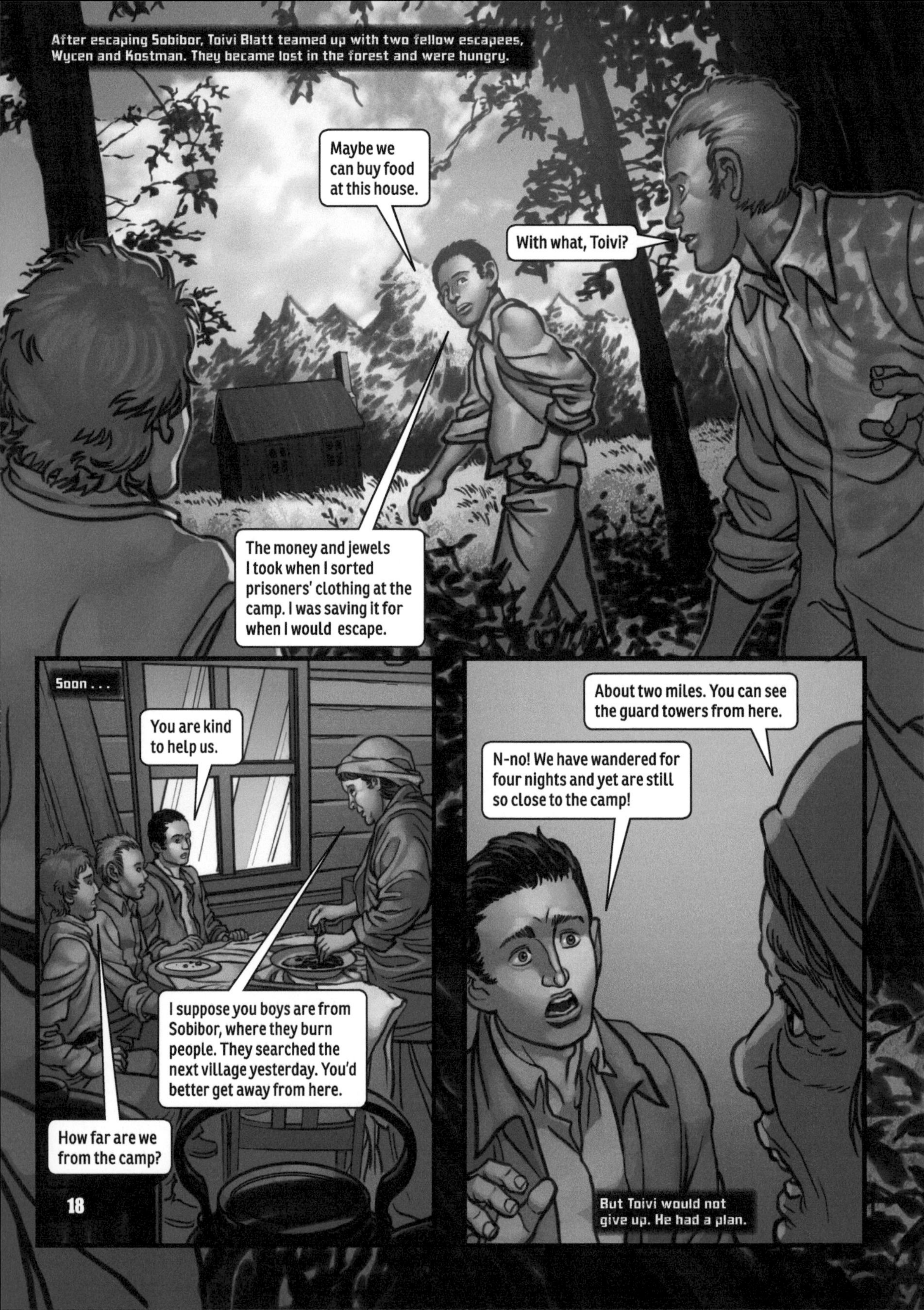

After escaping Sobibor, Toivi Blatt teamed up with two fellow escapees, Wycen and Kostman. They became lost in the forest and were hungry.
Maybe we can buy food at this house.
With what, Toivi?
The money and jewels I took when I sorted prisoners' clothing at the camp. I was saving it for when I would escape.
Soon . . .
You are kind to help us.
I suppose you boys are from Sobibor, where they burn people. They searched the next village yesterday. You'd better get away from here.
How far are we from the camp?
About two miles. You can see the guard towers from here.
N-no! We have wandered for four nights and yet are still so close to the camp!
But Toivi would not give up. He had a plan.

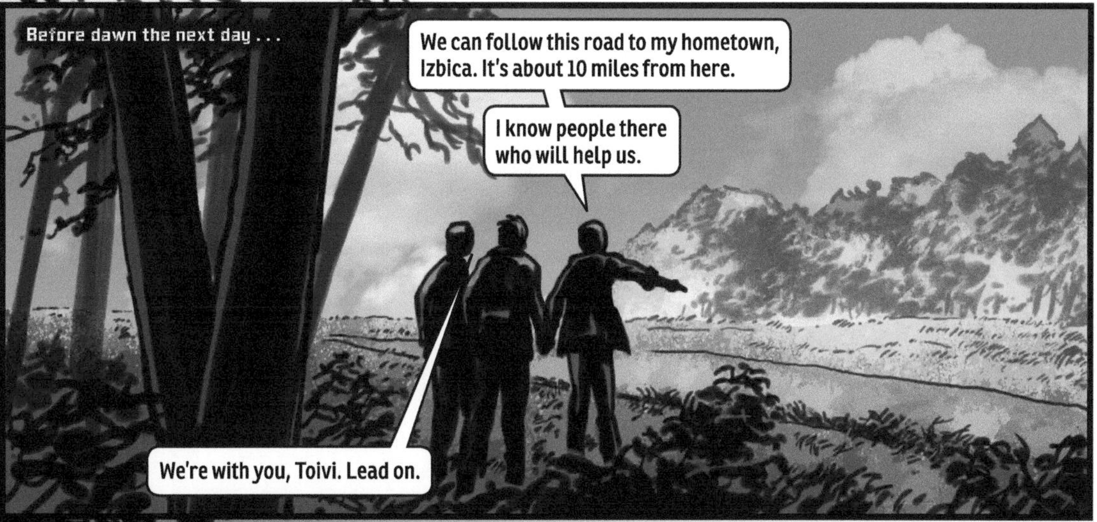
Before dawn the next day . . .
We can follow this road to my hometown, Izbica. It's about 10 miles from here.
I know people there who will help us.
We're with you, Toivi. Lead on.

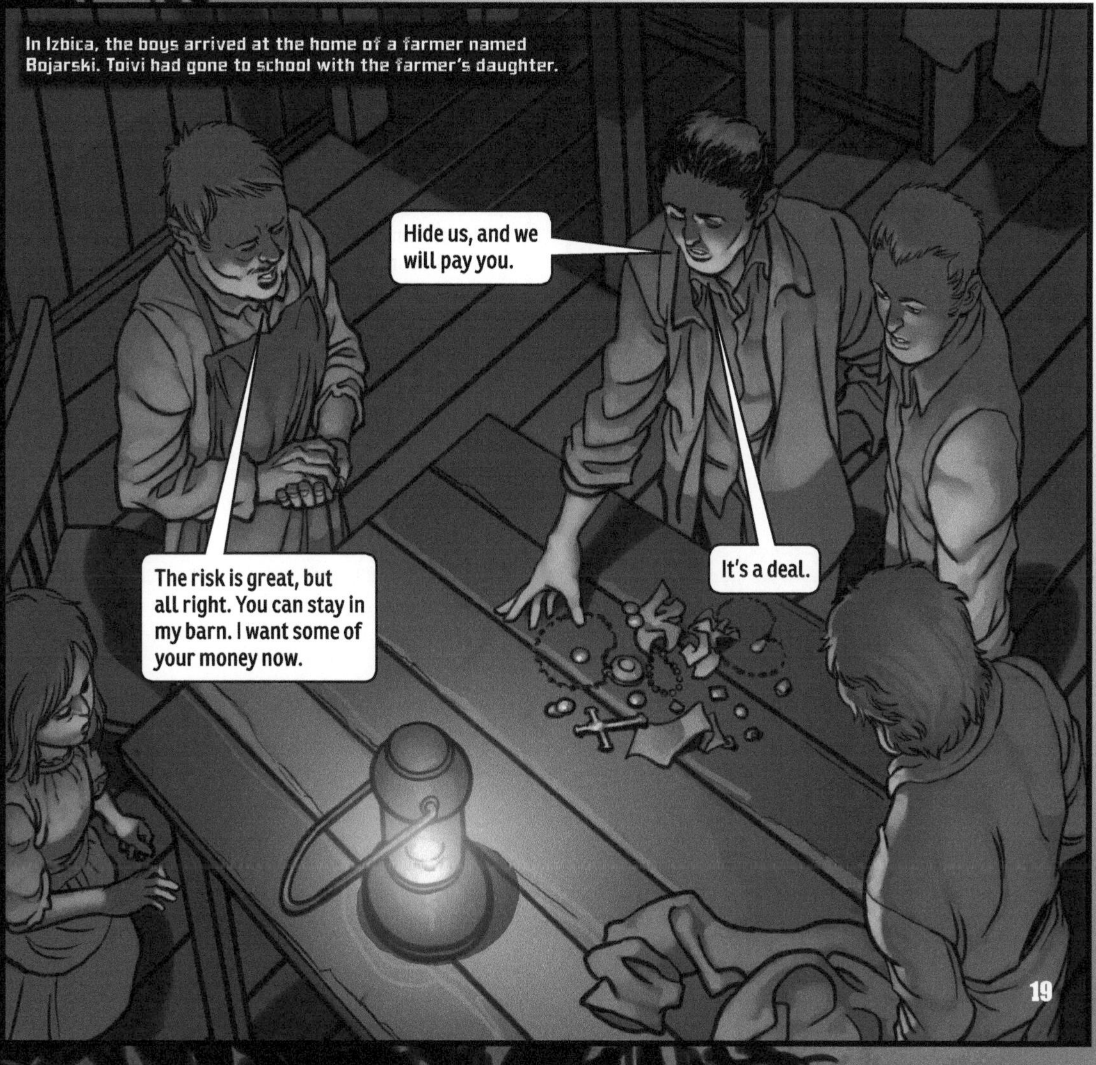
In Izbica, the boys arrived at the home of a farmer named Bojarski. Toivi had gone to school with the farmer's daughter.
Hide us, and we will pay you.
The risk is great, but all right. You can stay in my barn. I want some of your money now.
It's a deal.

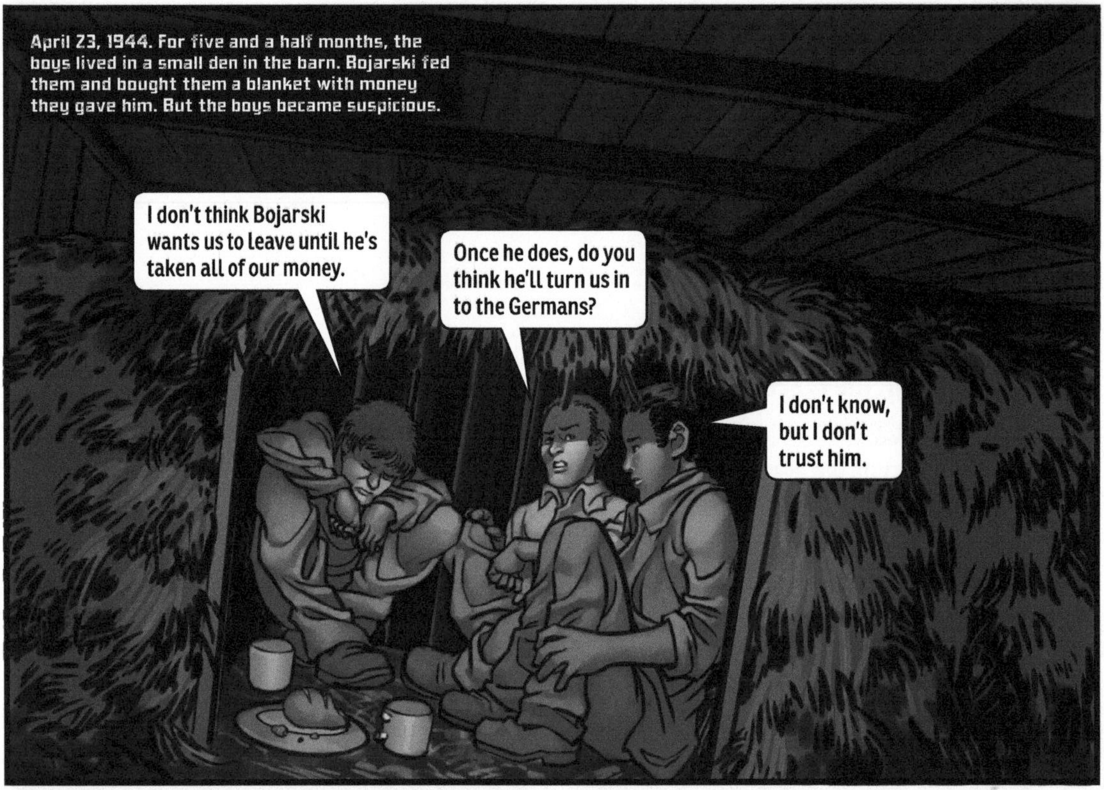
April 23, 1944. For five and a half months, the boys lived in a small den in the barn. Bojarski fed them and bought them a blanket with money they gave him. But the boys became suspicious.
I don't think Bojarski wants us to leave until he's taken all of our money.
Once he does, do you think he'll turn us in to the Germans?
I don't know, but I don't trust him.

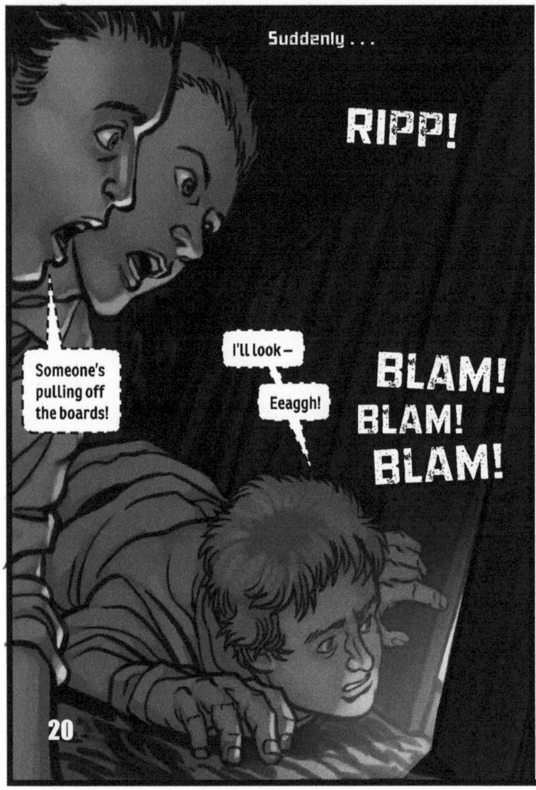
Suddenly . . .
RIPP!
Someone's pulling off the boards!
I'll look—
Eeaggh!
BLAM!
BLAM!
BLAM!

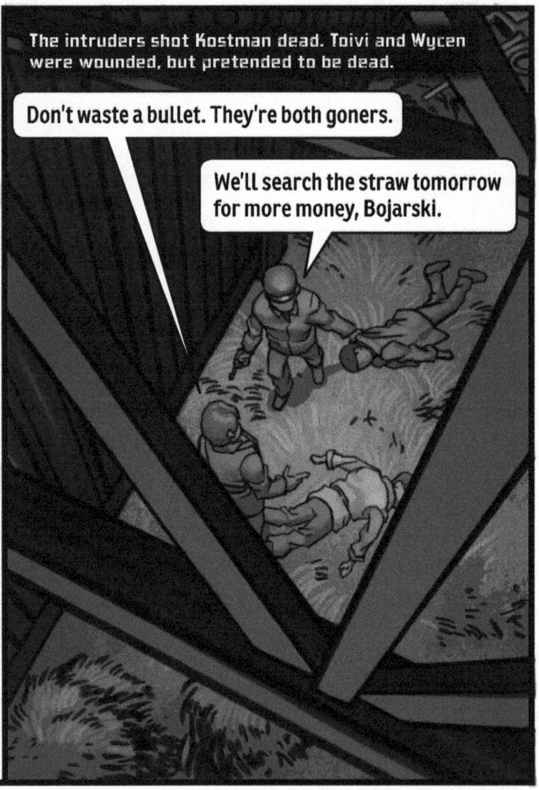
The intruders shot Kostman dead. Toivi and Wycen were wounded, but pretended to be dead.
Don't waste a bullet. They're both goners.
We'll search the straw tomorrow for more money, Bojarski.

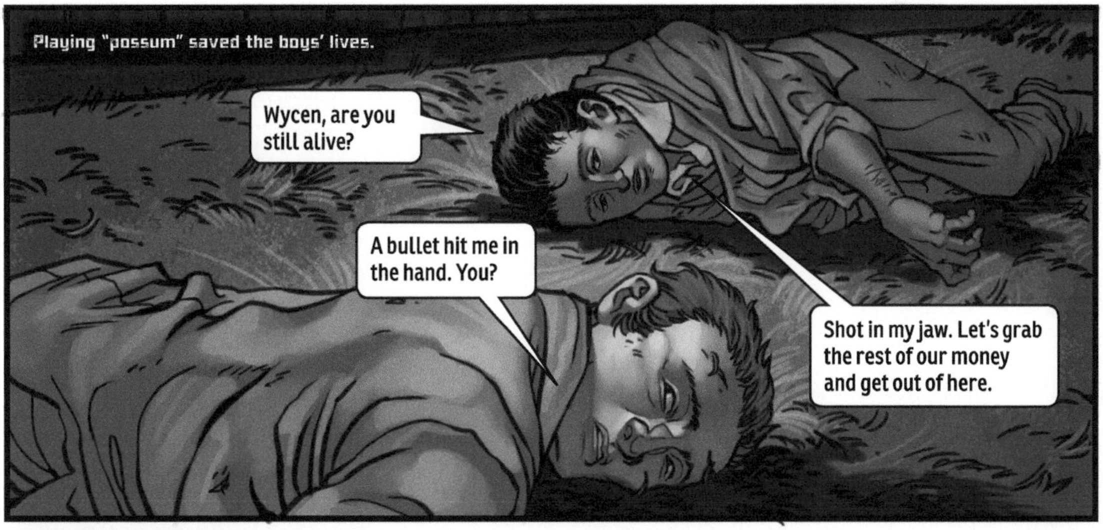
Playing "possum" saved the boys' lives.
Wycen, are you still alive?
A bullet hit me in the hand. You?
Shot in my jaw. Let's grab the rest of our money and get out of here.

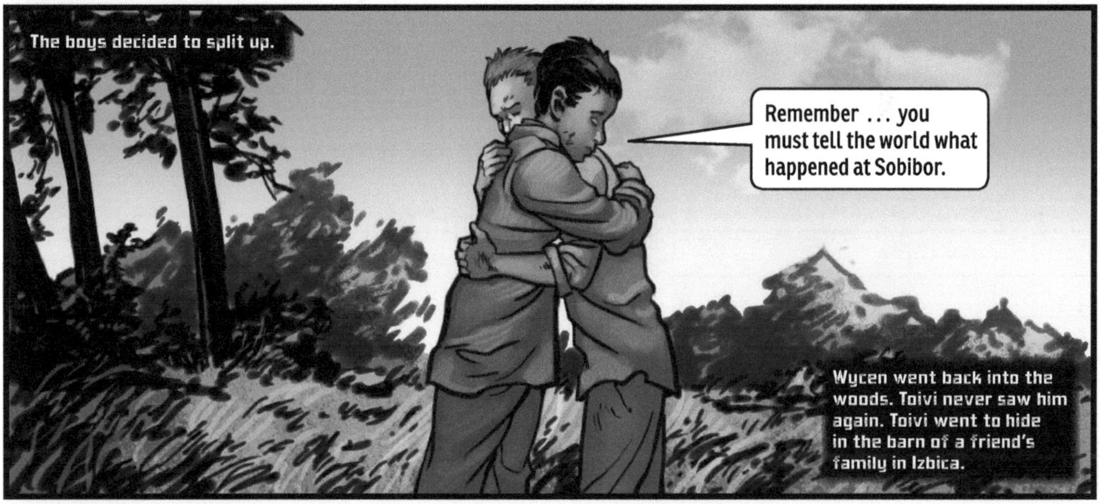
The boys decided to split up.
Remember . . . you must tell the world what happened at Sobibor.
Wycen went back into the woods. Toivi never saw him again. Toivi went to hide in the barn of a friend's family in Izbica.

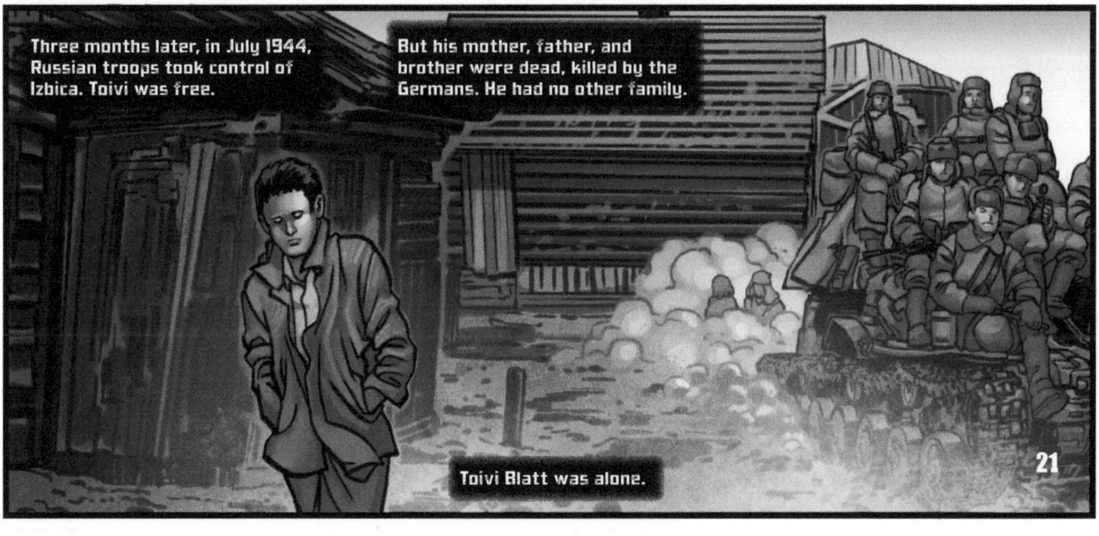
Three months later, in July 1944, Russian troops took control of Izbica. Toivi was free.
But his mother, father, and brother were dead, killed by the Germans. He had no other family.
Toivi Blatt was alone.

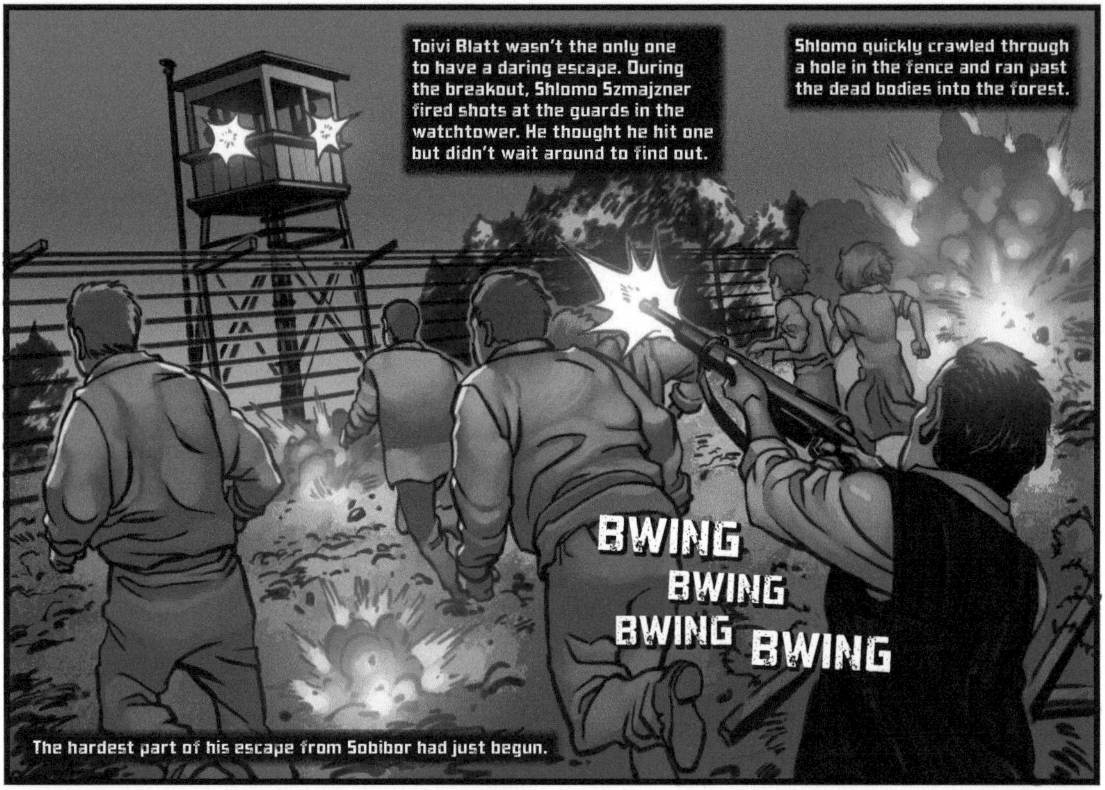
Toivi Blatt wasn't the only one to have a daring escape. During the breakout, Shlomo Szmajzner fired shots at the guards in the watchtower. He thought he hit one but didn't wait around to find out.
Shlomo quickly crawled through a hole in the fence and ran past the dead bodies into the forest.
BWING
BWING
BWING
BWING
The hardest part of his escape from Sobibor had just begun.

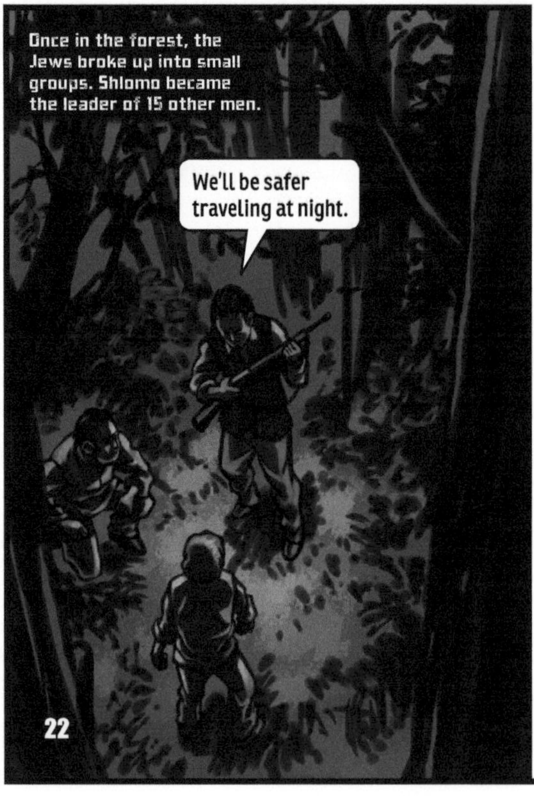
Once in the forest, the Jews broke up into small groups. Shlomo became the leader of 15 other men.
We'll be safer traveling at night.

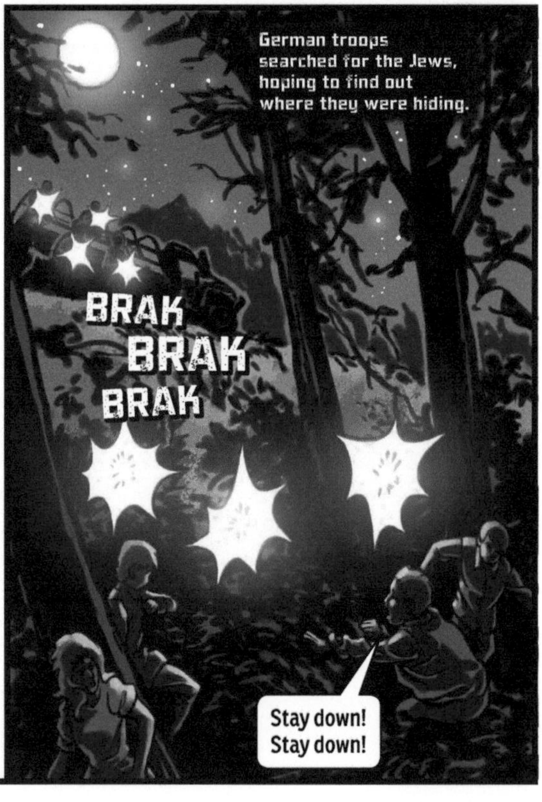
German troops searched for the Jews, hoping to find out where they were hiding.
BRAK
BRAK
BRAK
Stay down! Stay down!

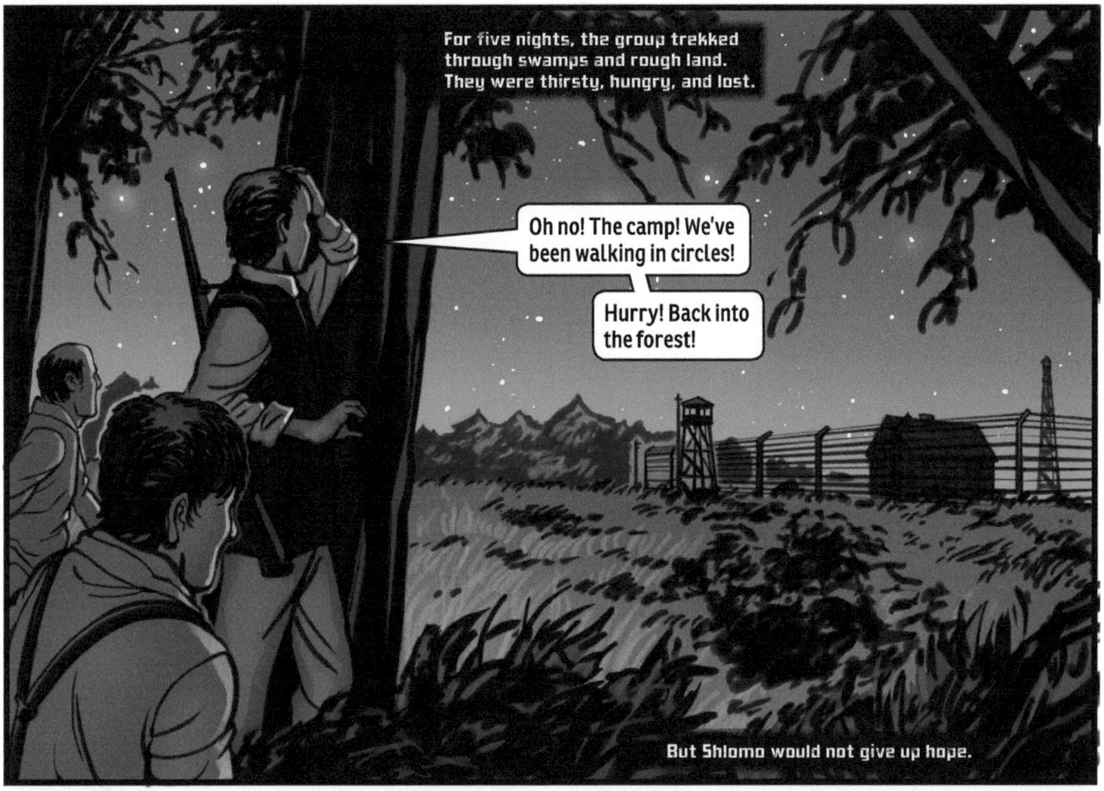
For five nights, the group trekked through swamps and rough land. They were thirsty, hungry, and lost.
Oh no! The camp! We've been walking in circles!
Hurry! Back into the forest!
But Shlomo would not give up hope.

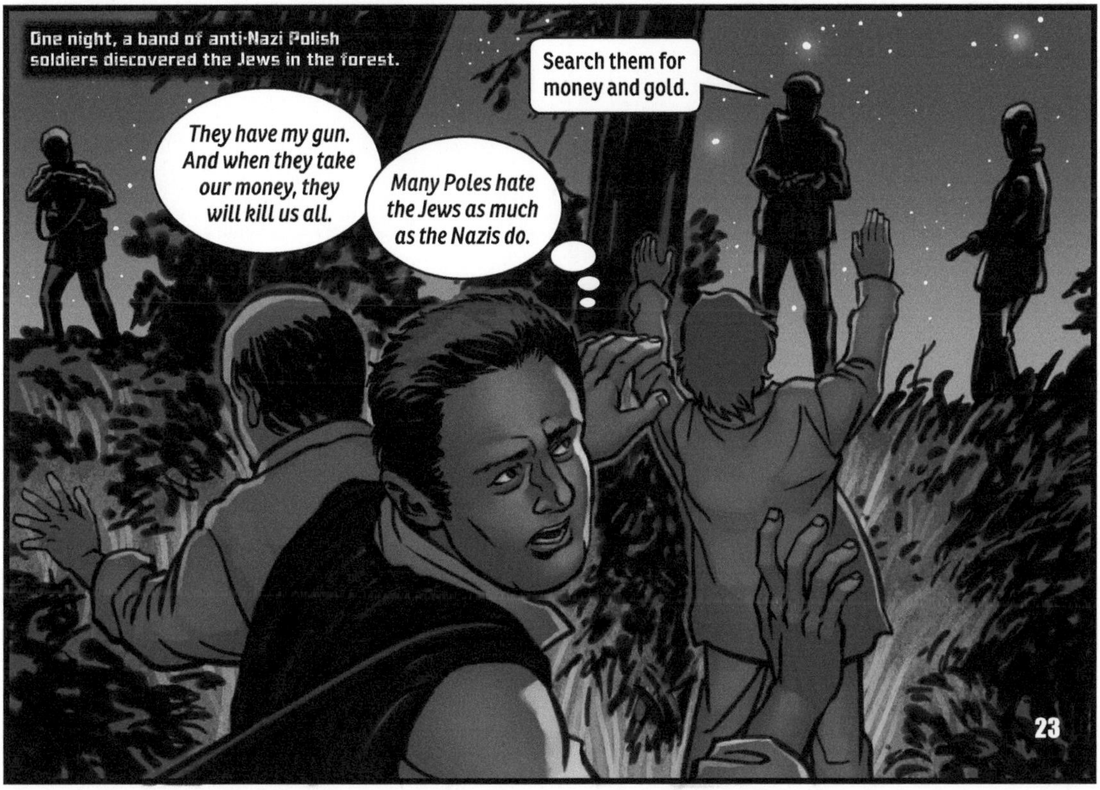
One night, a band of anti-Nazi Polish soldiers discovered the Jews in the forest.
Search them for money and gold.
They have my gun. And when they take our money, they will kill us all.
Many Poles hate the Jews as much as the Nazis do.

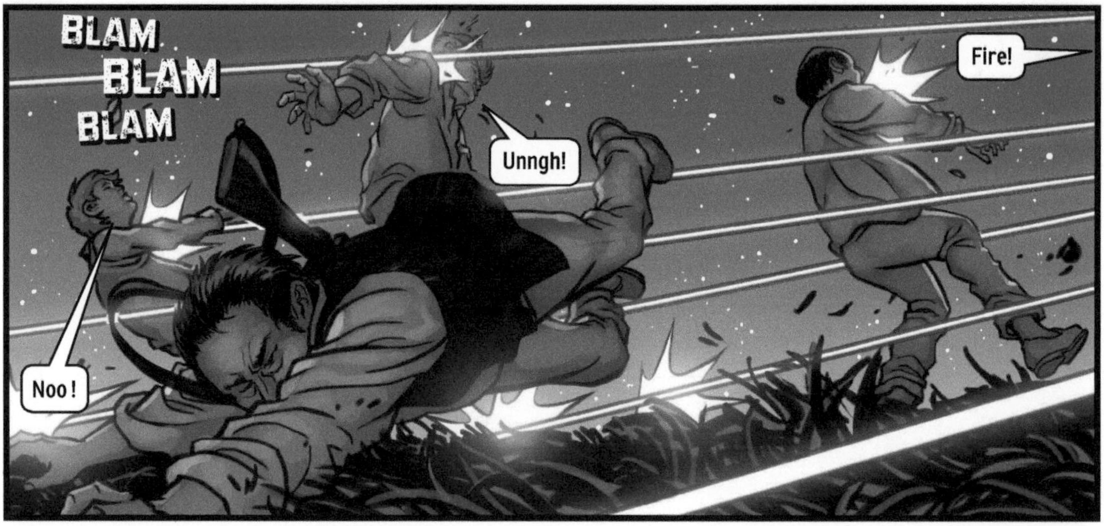
BLAM
BLAM
BLAM
Unngh!
Fire!
Noo!

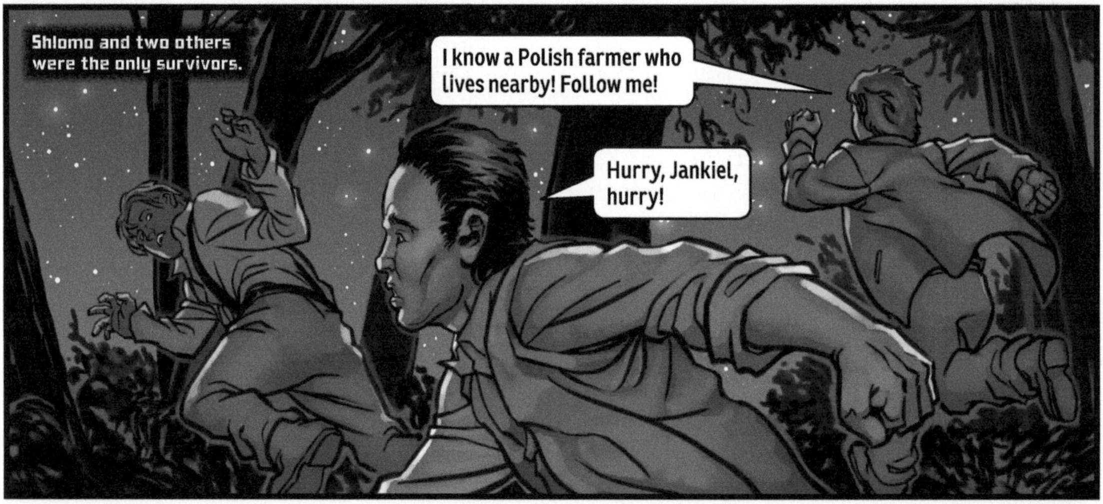
Shlomo and two others were the only survivors.
I know a Polish farmer who lives nearby! Follow me!
Hurry, Jankiel, hurry!

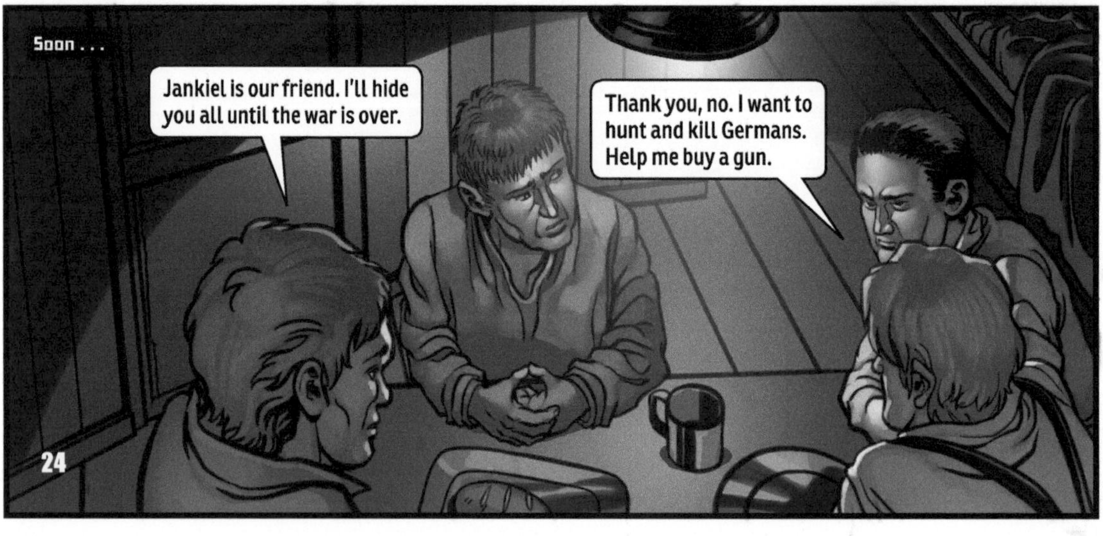
Soon . . .
Jankiel is our friend. I'll hide you all until the war is over.
Thank you, no. I want to hunt and kill Germans. Help me buy a gun.

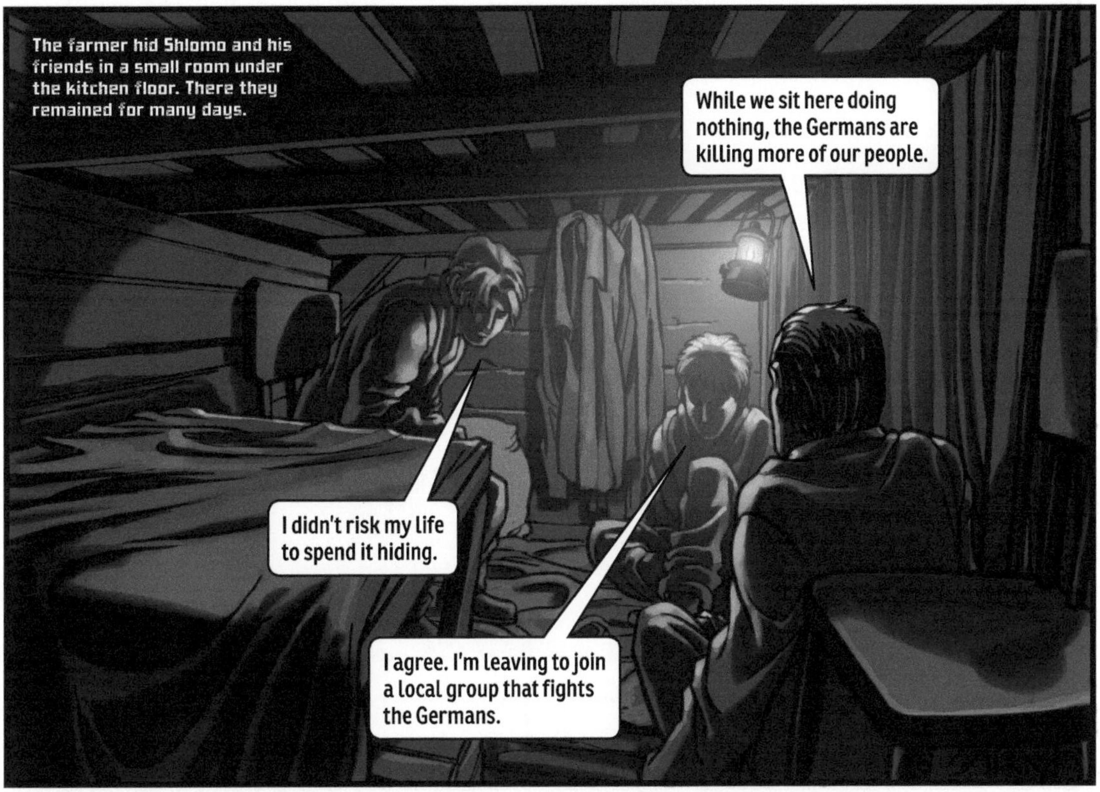
The farmer hid Shlomo and his friends in a small room under the kitchen floor. There they remained for many days.
While we sit here doing nothing, the Germans are killing more of our people.
I didn't risk my life to spend it hiding.
I agree. I'm leaving to join a local group that fights the Germans.

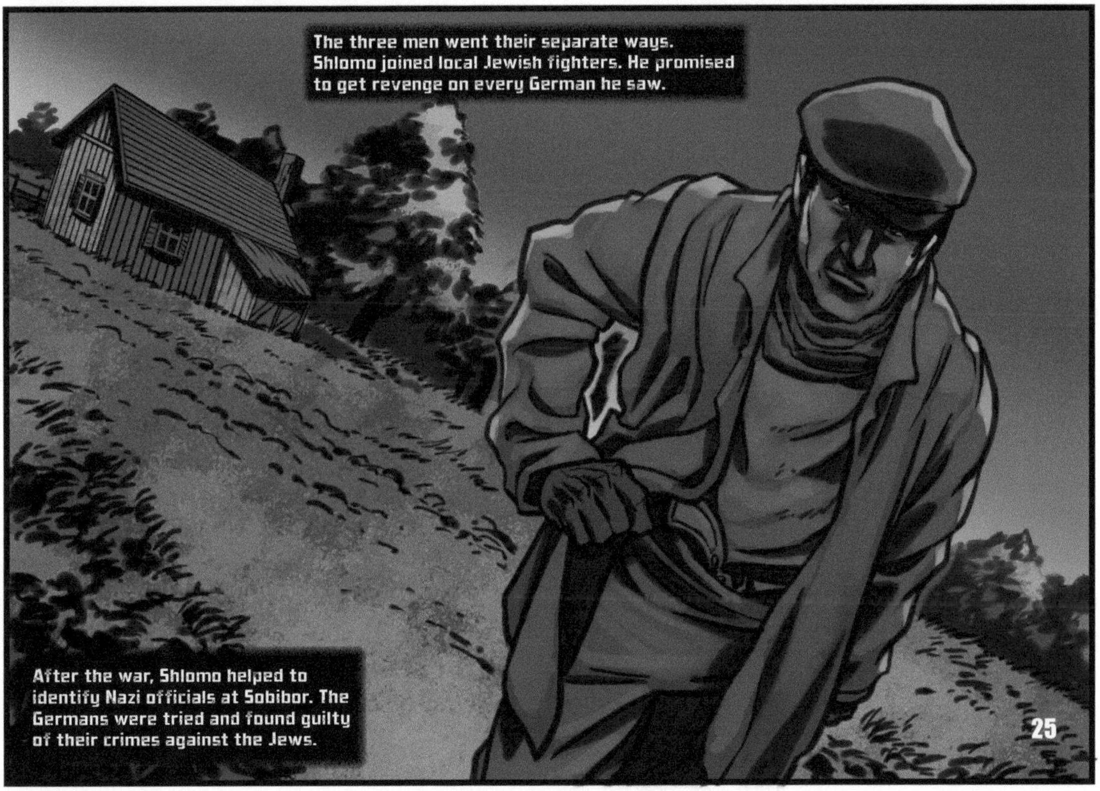
The three men went their separate ways. Shlomo joined local Jewish fighters. He promised to get revenge on every German he saw.
After the war, Shlomo helped to identify Nazi officials at Sobibor. The Germans were tried and found guilty of their crimes against the Jews.

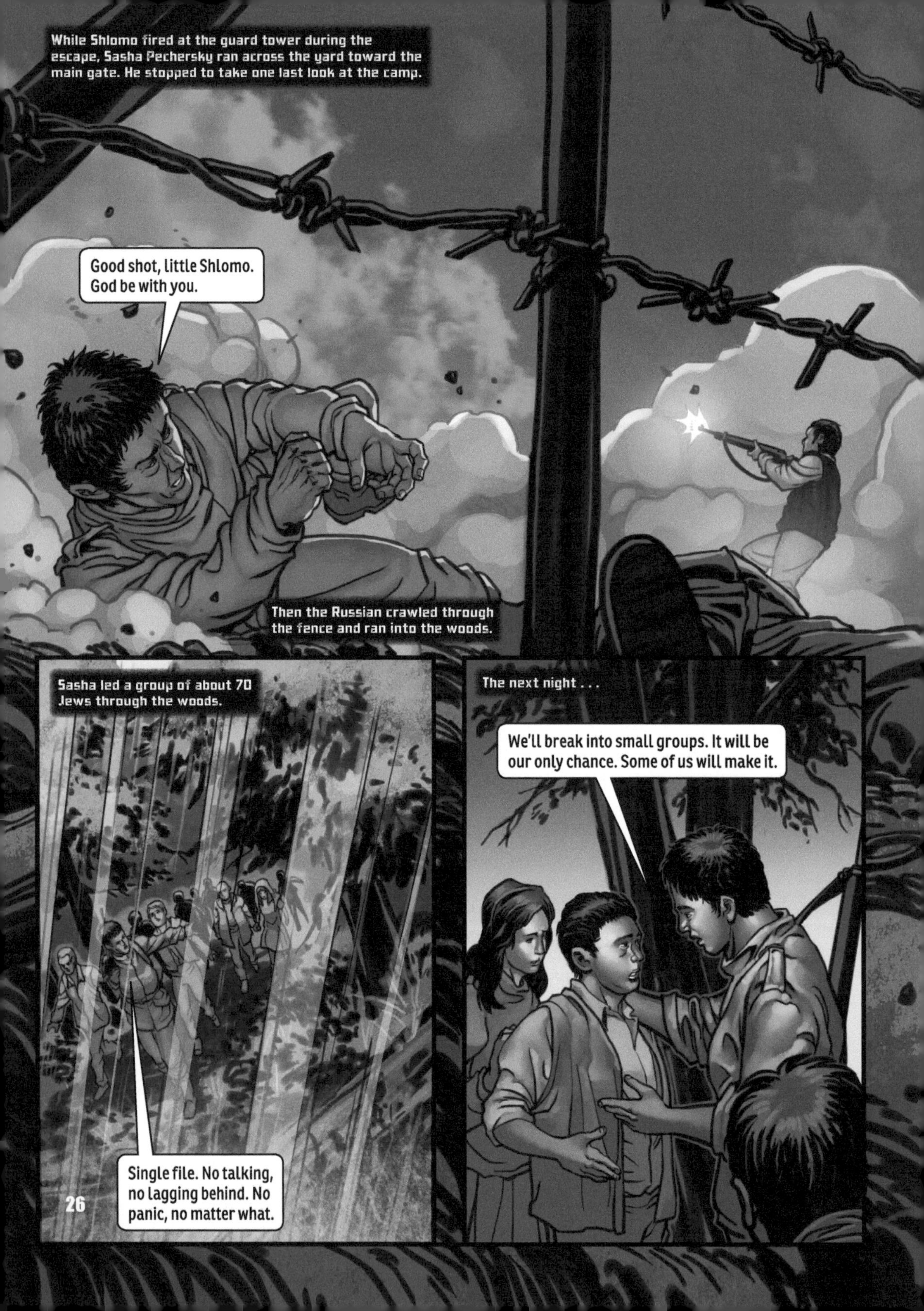
While Shlomo fired at the guard tower during the escape, Sasha Pechersky ran across the yard toward the main gate. He stopped to take one last look at the camp.
Good shot, little Shlomo. God be with you.
Then the Russian crawled through the fence and ran into the woods.
Sasha led a group of about 70 Jews through the woods.
Single file. No talking, no lagging behind. No panic, no matter what.
The next night . . .
We'll break into small groups. It will be our only chance. Some of us will make it.

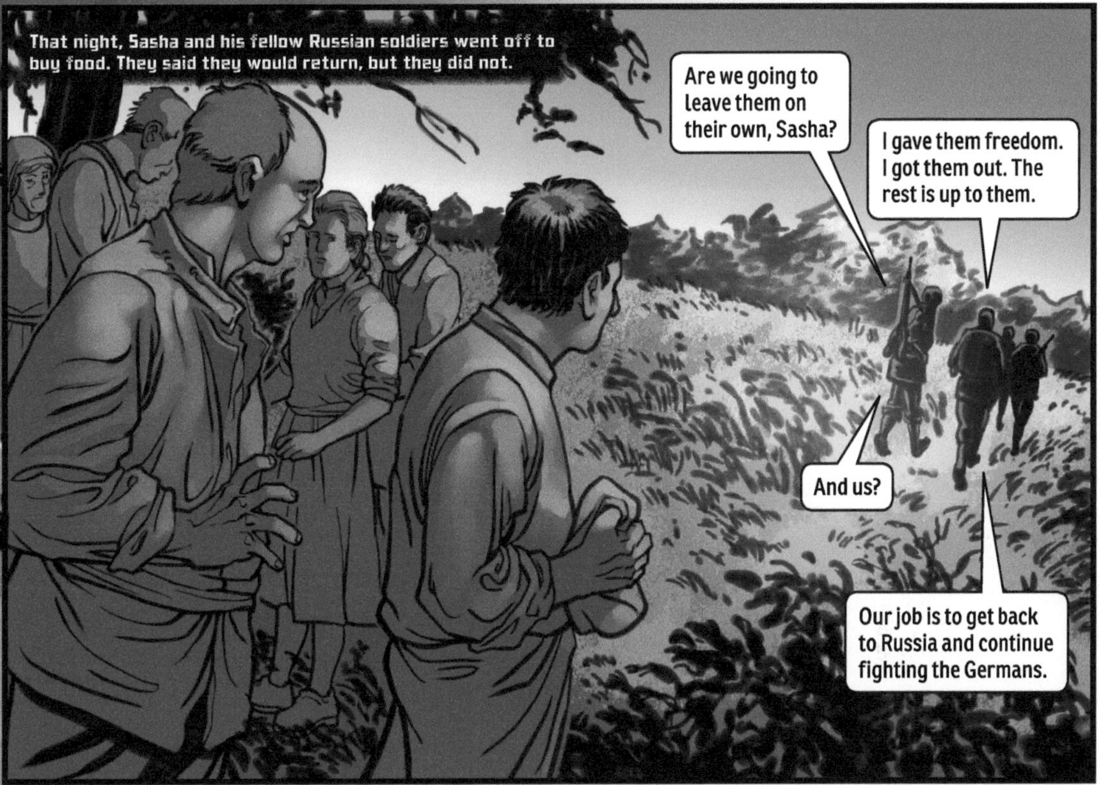
That night, Sasha and his fellow Russian soldiers went off to buy food. They said they would return, but they did not.
Are we going to leave them on their own, Sasha?
I gave them freedom. I got them out. The rest is up to them.
And us?
Our job is to get back to Russia and continue fighting the Germans.

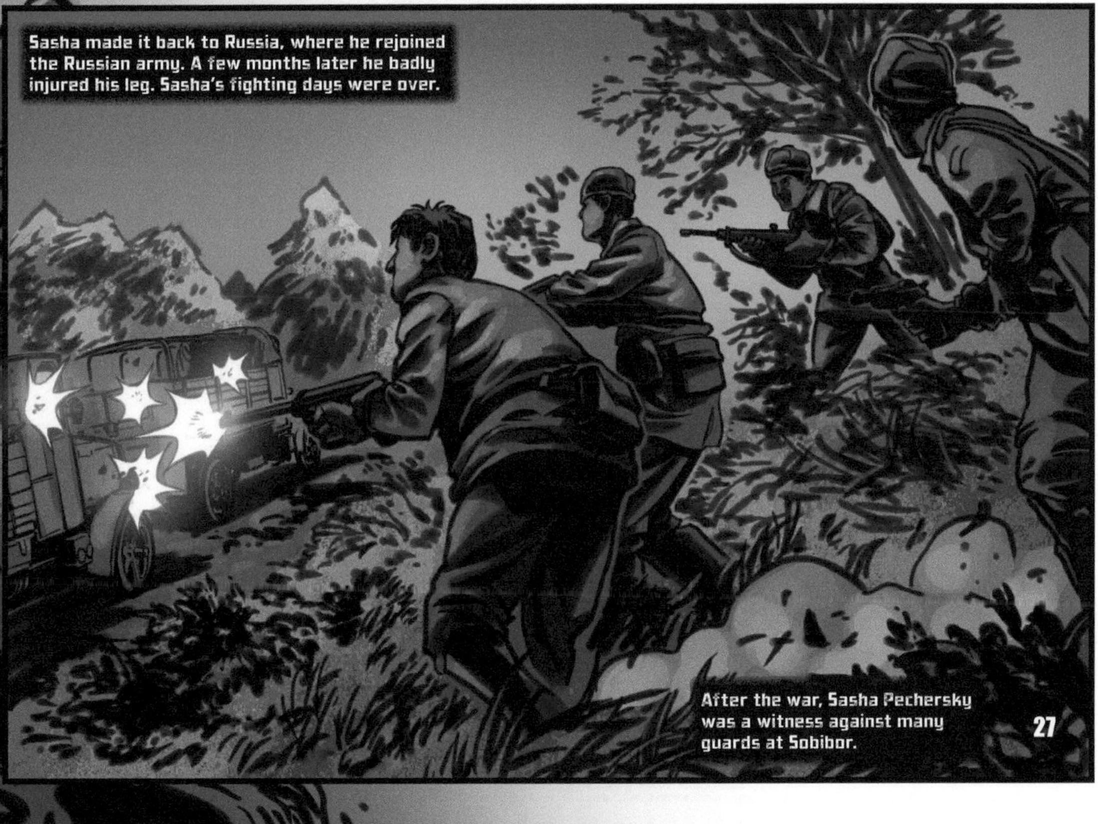
Sasha made it back to Russia, where he rejoined the Russian army. A few months later he badly injured his leg. Sasha's fighting days were over.
After the war, Sasha Pechersky was a witness against many guards at Sobibor.

THE NIGHTMARE IS OVER

In October 1943, roughly 600 prisoners were left in the Sobibor death camp. About 300 men and women managed to break out on October 14. About 50 men and women made it to freedom and managed to survive the war. The others were captured and killed by the Germans, local Poles, and Polish anti-Nazi fighting groups. Leon Feldhendler successfully escaped, but was killed in a robbery in Lublin, Poland, in April 1945.

After the breakout, in October 1943, the Germans took apart the camp. The entire area was planted with trees to erase all evidence of the horrors that took place there. The remaining Jewish prisoners who did not escape were shot.

In 1965–1966, trials were held for the German officials who ran the camp. Six men were found guilty of participating in the mass murder of tens of thousands of Jews at Sobibor. Each received a jail sentence, including Karl

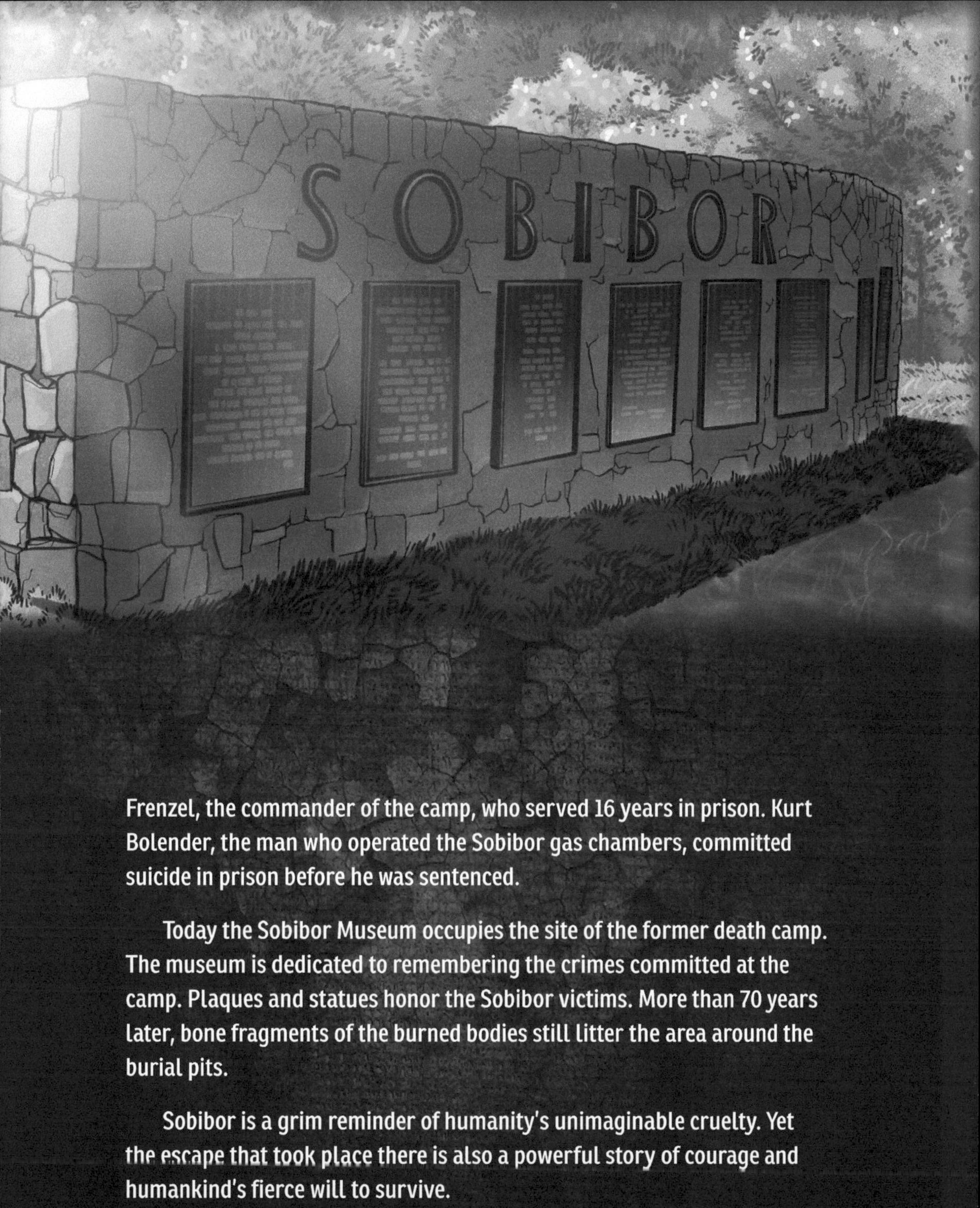
SOBIBOR

Frenzel, the commander of the camp, who served 16 years in prison. Kurt Bolender, the man who operated the Sobibor gas chambers, committed suicide in prison before he was sentenced.

Today the Sobibor Museum occupies the site of the former death camp. The museum is dedicated to remembering the crimes committed at the camp. Plaques and statues honor the Sobibor victims. More than 70 years later, bone fragments of the burned bodies still litter the area around the burial pits.

Sobibor is a grim reminder of humanity's unimaginable cruelty. Yet the escape that took place there is also a powerful story of courage and humankind's fierce will to survive.

GLOSSARY

ammunition (am-yuh-NISH-uhn)—things such as bullets or shells that can be fired from weapons

armory (AHR-mur-ee)—a place where weapons are stored

barracks (BAR-uhks)—a large building or group of buildings where soldiers are housed

carbon monoxide (KAHR-buhn muh-NAK-side)—a colorless and odorless poisonous gas

concentration camp (KAHN-suhn-tray-shun KAMP)—a place where large numbers of prisoners are kept, sometimes to await mass execution

escapees (ih-SKAPE-eez)—people who have escaped from somewhere

intruders (in-TROO-durs)—people who break into buildings to steal things or harm people inside

minefields (MINE-feeldz)—areas planted with explosive mines

Nazi (NAHT-see)—the political group that ruled Germany from 1933 to 1945; Adolph Hitler was the group's leader

roll call (ROHL KAWL)—the reading aloud of a list of names to determine who is present

witness (WIT-nis)—a person who gives evidence in a court of law

CRITICAL THINKING
USING THE COMMON CORE

1. Put yourself in the place of a prisoner who escaped from Sobibor. Would you want to try to reach freedom on your own, or would you choose instead to travel with a large group of fellow escapees? Use the prisoners' experiences from the text to support your answer.

2. The Jewish escapees must have felt many different emotions as they fled Sobibor: fear, joy, excitement, uncertainty, and more. Describe a personal event in your life that caused you to experience a variety of emotions.

3. Suppose you were a high-ranking officer in the U.S. military and learned about the horrors of the Nazi death camps. What would you do?

READ MORE

Guillain, Charlotte. *Great Escapes.* War Stories. Chicago: Heinemann Library, 2012.

Hodge, Deborah. *Rescuing the Children: The Story of the Kindertransport.* Toronto: Tundra Books, 2012.

Peppas, Lynn. *The Holocaust.* Uncovering the Past: Analyzing Primary Sources. New York: Crabtree Publishing Company, 2015.

Woolf, Alex. *Children of the Holocaust.* Hauppauge, N.Y.: Barron's, 2014.

INTERNET SITES

FactHound offers a safe, fun way to find Internet sites related to this book. All sites on FactHound have been researched by our staff.

Here's all you do:

Visit *www.facthound.com*

Type in this code: 9781515735328

 Super-cool stuff! Check out projects, games and lots more at **www.capstonekids.com**

INDEX

TITLES IN THIS SET

BEHIND ENEMY LINES:
The Escape of Robert Grimes with the Comet Line

DEATH CAMP UPRISING:
The Escape from Sobibor Concentration Camp

OUTRUNNING THE NAZIS:
The Brave Escape of Resistance Fighter Sven Somme

TUNNELING TO FREEDOM:
The Great Escape from Stalag Luft III